BUDDHISM

BUDD

HISM

on the path to nirvana

Text: Swati Chopra

Foreword: Professor Lokesh Chandra

BRIJBASI

contents

A - 81, Sector V, Noida - 2013301
Uttar Pradesh, India

First published by Brijbasi Art Press Ltd. 2005

Text: Swati Chopra
Editor: Shalini Saran
Photo Editor: Lance Dane
Project Editor: Veena Baswani
Design: Yogesh Suraksha Design Studio. w.w.w. ysdesignstudio.com
Research: Sundeep Bali

ISBN 81-87902-17-5

Processed at Brijbasi Art Press Ltd.
E - 46/11, Okhla Industrial Area Phase II, New Delhi - 110020, India

PICTURE CREDITS

The publishers would like to express their appreciation to the photographers, museums and archives for kindly permitting the reproduction of their works and for their support. Every effort has been made to obtain and fulfil the copyright for all the images depicted in the book. However, should there be any further claims, the individuals concerned may kindly approach the publisher.

(a-above, b-bottom, t-top, c-centre, l-left, r-right, e-extreme)

Lance Dane: 1, 4L, 4TR, 5TL, 5TC, 5TR (Pan Asian Collection), 5BR, 5BC, 5BL, 6, 13T, 13B, 14-15, 16TR, 17TL, 17BR, 18 (courtesy National Museum, New Delhi), 19, 22, 23B (courtesy Private Collection), 25, 26-27, 27BR, 28, 35B, 41BR, 42T, 42R, 43TL, 43TR, 44R, 44L, 45T, 45BR, 45BL, 47T, 48-49, 50A, 52A, 52-53BC, 53T, 54, 56B, 62TL, 62BR, 62-63TC, 65T, 65BR, 66-67, 69T, 69BR, 70R, 70B, 71L, 71B, 76T, 76B, 79, 83, 85T, 85B, 86-87, 88T, 88BR, 92R (courtesy Desmond Doig), 92BL, 93L, 93A, 95, 97, 100T, 100B, 101T, 101B, 103BR, 109T, 109B, 111, 112T, 113L, 113B (courtesy national Museum, New Delhi), 116, 117L, 117BR, 118L (courtesy National Museum, New Delhi), 119TL, 121BR, 122-123 (courtesy Madras Museum), 125, 126B, 130BL, 132BL, 133BR, 134-135, 136BL,137, 139T, 139BR, 141BR, 142T, 142B (courtesy ASI), 144L, 145, 150B, 151B, 153, 154, 155BR, Back cover

Dinodia: Front cover - Ashvin Mehta, 12, 24, 34, 35T - P. A. Acharya, 41TL - N. G. Sharma, 46 - Nrupen Madhvani, 50T, 56T - Ashvin Mehta, 72-73 - Sunil S. Kapadia, 84, 104-105, 114-115 - B. P. Maiti, 124T, 124B, 130T, 131T, 131BR, 136T - S. Nagaraj, 143T - Bharat Damani, 143BL - Nrupen Madhvani

Ashok Dilwali: 2-3, 63B, 90, 91, 102T, 102B, 108, 127

Victoria & Albert Museum: 4BR

Thomas Kelly: 8-9, 20-21, 33, 37, 51, 58-59, 64, 68, 78, 80-81, 82, 96, 103, 106TL, 106TR, 106B, 107T, 107B, 121TL, 126T, 133TL, 143BR, 144TR, 151T, 155, 158-159

Rajesh Bedi: 10-11, 38-39, 40, 74-75, 98-99, 148-149

Bharat Kala Bhavan: 16BL

Archaeological Survey of India: 23T, 30, 32

Sanjay Acharya: 29, 36, 57, 60-61, 94T, 95B, 120, 128-129, 146-147, 150T, 156-157

Archivio White Star: 31 - Marcello Bertinetti

National Museum: 42AL, 47R, 132TL

British Museum: 52T

Shalini Saran: 53B

Private Collection: 55, 112BL, 100-101BC, 138, 140-141

Cleveland Museum: 77, 110-111

Prakash Israni: 103TR, 119TR

Dr. Shashibala: 121TR, 160

Indian Museum, Kolkata: 132-133BC

PAGE 6
Gandharan style Buddha Sakyamuni, c. 2nd-3rd century, probably from Afghanistan. The demeanour is one of grace and serenity.

PAGE 1: The *dharmacakra hasta* is a hand gesture where the thumb and the first finger touch to make a circle, and the other fingers rest alongside.
It symbolises the *dharma-cakra-pravartana* – the Wheel of Law. Such iconographic *mudras,* hand gestures, enhanced the spoken word, providing authority to a Buddha or bodhisattva image.

PAGES 2-3: A symbol of the Buddha in early Buddhist art, Buddhist thought likens the human heart to an unopened lotus – when one realises one's innate Buddhahood, the lotus blossoms.

PAGE 4, L: An angry form of the bodhisattva Majushri; Nepal, 10th century, gilt copper with paint. Striking a militant pose known as *alidha,* his right hand holds a sword, of which only the hilt now remains.

PAGE 4, TR: A bodhisattva, probably Maitreya, Gandhara School, 2nd century. The nimbus around the head is symbolic of enlightenment.

PAGE 4, BR: A steatite reliquary portraying animals in its panels.

PAGE 5, TL: Holding a sword aloft, this variation of Manjushri is from Nalanda, c. 12th-13th century.

PAGE 5, TC: This 7th century sculpture from Korea shows Maitreya in a pensive mood.

PAGE 5, TR: A gilt copper image of the Buddha Sakyamuni from Burma, c. 12th-13th century. His right hand touches the earth, the silent witness of his enlightenment, in a *bhumisparsa mudra.*
The face is somewhat square and the nose unusually aquiline.

PAGE 5, BR: A smile that lights the world – a Kushan Buddha made of sandstone, c. 2nd-3rd century.

PAGE 5, BC: A standing Buddha coin portraying the golden dinnar legend BODDO.

PAGE 5, BL: Maitreya carries a pot containing the elixir of life in this elegant gilded Nepal sculpture, c. 9th century.

Pages 8-9: A young monk distributes sacred cords blessed by H. H. the Dalai Lama at the Kalachakra Initiation in Bodhgaya.
The Dalai Lama has now made this an annual event, and often presides over the ceremony himself.

Pages 10-11: Stag dance in honour of Lord Mahakala, the Great Destroyer, performed by members of the Tibetan Karma Kagyu (also known as the Red Hat after their headgear) sect. Animistic rituals such as this are probably vestiges of Bon, the pre-Buddhist, shamanastic faith of Tibet.

FOREWORD

This book is an effort to distil centuries of Buddhism, its insights into ultimate reality, its colourful imagery, its pristine lucidity of the pure seed of Buddhahood that resides in the heart of all beings, or in the words of yogini Kambala:

Lotus pollen wakes up in the heart's centre.
The bright flower is free from mud.

Swati Chopra, the author of the book, gathers the essences of many flowers and blends them into an all-encompassing presentation so that we may comprehend the life of Lord Buddha, His Enlightenment, His ministry, and the blossoming of Buddhism around the world.

In the volume of skylike emptiness, to
Write with letters of pure awareness and wisdom.

The Buddha is neither a messenger of God nor of Revelation, but is supremely human. He attained *bodhi* through strenuous effort and preached a message of universal validity, to awaken the spirit that dwells in the inner being of all people. He spent the last monsoon of his life at Venuvana on the outskirts of Vaishali. Resting under a tree he remarked: 'This world is beautiful – it is a joy to live in it.' Leaving Vaishali, he journeyed with Ananda, stayed at Pava where he dined at the house of Chunda, with dire consequences, leading to his *parinirvana*. The prime concern of Buddhism is with human and other sentient beings, while in other faiths the response is to a god or gods. The Buddha felt a deep affinity with nature: he pre-incarnated as different animals or king-trees in the Jatakas. A tree is life, an animal is life, nature is our brother. A Japanese poem begins: 'O pine, O my brother . . .' Only in Buddhism can a pine be a brother.

Buddhist values are founded in a humane, spiritual mind-ground, in the integrity of our consciousness, and in a commitment to life. *Dukha*, sadness, is the negative space of life, imperfections of all kinds, whose cessation is nirvana. It is a way to experience the nobility of life without the intervention of concepts. Today we stand at the threshold of the imbalance of the biosphere of our inheritance and the technosphere of our creation. The global crisis is *dukha*. This book is meant to arouse in us the unfolding of the Way in all its grandeur of thought, the multiple textures of the sangha, its cosmopolis across the vast spaces of Asia, winds of the immortals caressing the brush and the burin in paintings and sculpture, or the *sunyata* and *rupam* in the caves, symbolic tangents of what takes place in the gardens of transcendence. This book weaves and unweaves the webs of Buddhism wherein humans are in essence ever becoming, yonder-farers in the beyond, or as the Heart Sutra says: *Gate gate para-sangate bodhi suaha*.

The author seeks to sow precious seeds in the hearts of her readers, intending them to grow into strong, healthy *bodhi* trees whose branches will blow soft breezes into the heart of humankind, so that:

Dwelling in tranquillity,
Seeing the dharma, returning to the source,
Without hatred or violence
Joy and peace overflow.

This book should be a lotus in our hands, and we, seeker bodhisattvas, looking beyond the eyes and the mind, surrounded by infinities and transfinities.

Lokesh Chandra

PROFESSOR LOKESH CHANDRA

THE BUDDHA

In the space of the two and a half millennia that separate him from us, much has been said, written and argued about the man who came to be known as Gautama the Buddha. Founder of the path to self-awareness that we today know as Buddhism, he has been mythified, deified and exalted. Buddhist scriptures, which began to be written a couple of centuries after he died, eventually projected the Buddha as a godly being with miraculous powers of perception, and already destined for nirvana at birth.

This superheroic persona is further enhanced by the legends that wove themselves around the man and his life as time went by. One example is the story of his wondrous birth, appearing from his mother's side rather than through the birth canal. Also, his liberation is said to have been a pre-ordained phenomenon brought on through lifetimes of preparation as a bodhisattva, a Buddha-to-be, instead of insights gathered through intense, but human contemplation in a normal, single lifetime.

While mythology has its place in culture and religion, its proclivity for glorification might, at times, obscure what really happened. This happened in the case of the Buddha, the humanness of whose quest is compromised in order to present him as an almighty all-knower. And it happened, perhaps, to lend his teaching greater authority in the eyes of the common man and woman in the times after his death, when his followers were attempting to plant the Buddha's dharma in the popular mindset as another religion.

So, who was this man? How did he come to be the Awakened One? Was he really a spiritual superman, or was he a regular human being who sought and discovered a truth?

The answers lie somewhere along the ancient-modern path that he traversed, which even though swirling with thoughts, perceptions

FACING PAGE: Child lamas in a monastery. The tradition of giving up one or two children to the local monastery was a way in which the monastic tradition was sustained in Tibet.

TOP: A detail from a finely illustrated palm-leaf manuscript, from the library of the Asiatic Society, Kolkata. This is an example of the skilful penmanship and coloured visuals inspired by numerous Buddhist cannonical works preserved in monastic libraries in renowned Buddhist centres. They include the *Prajnaparimitre* (most popular in India and Nepal), a narrative of hierarchical images, the trials undergone prior to enlightenment, scenes of the eight miracles, and so on. Other examples are shown on pages 45, 63, 85, 109 and 139.

BOTTOM: The infant Buddha in a unique Kashmir copper sculpture. His birth in Lumbini denoted the fulfillment of the soothsayer's prophesy. It is believed that immediately after his birth, Siddhartha took seven steps unassisted, levitated and intoned: 'I alone am honoured in heaven and on the earth. This triple world is full of sufferings. I will be the saviour from these'. Seven lotus blossoms sprang from the earth in the footprints he had just made.

Queen Maya's Dream – a splendid Gandhara narrative sculpture, c. 2nd-3rd century, depicting Siddhartha's entry into her womb in the form of an elephant. This sculpture is noteworthy for its decorative Greek Corinthian pillars, the costumes of the guardians and attendants and its arches. Though Gandhara sculpture was influenced by Egyptian, Mongol, Greek, Scythian and Hebrew culture, among others, Buddhist religious influences predominated.

RIGHT: The remains of the Great Bharhut stupa built by Ashoka in 250 B. C. were excavated by Sir Alexander Cunningham in 1873. The earliest Buddhist extant monument of its kind, it was added to during the Sunga and Kushana periods. The Brahmi inscription above the medallion, 'Buddha, as the trumpeting elephant', announces his approach by blowing air through his trunk. Just before Buddha's birth, Queen Maya dreamt that a white elephant entered her womb. She is seen here, gowned and bejewelled, attended by maidens, one waving a whisk. The domestic ambience is created by the lamp. This railing pillar medallion is today preserved in the Indian Museum, Kolkata.

BOTTOM: A depiction by a Gandharan artist, c. 2nd century of Queen Maya holding on to a branch of the *sal* tree. The detail and refinement are characteristic of the sculpture of that period. Though only a fragment and therefore lacking other supportive detail to verify the identification, the posture and the regal bearing indicate an regal personage.

and beliefs of generations of believers, must retain the memory of the feet that first walked on it.

BIRTH AND EARLY LIFE

The Buddha was born Siddhartha Gautama in 563 B. C. to Suddhodhana, a chieftain of the Sakya clan, and his wife, Maya. Suddhodhana's state lay at the foothills of the Himalayas, with the bustling Kapilavastu as its capital. Later Buddhist texts ascribe the status of a great and very wealthy king to Suddhodhana, which was probably not so, since the state was a republic, and Suddhodhana an elected raja, ruler. Even so, Siddhartha was born into a life of comfort, with the possibility of succeeding his father, if he proved himself an able administrator.

Thoughts of governance were, however, far from young Siddhartha's mind. A pensive child, he would often remain immersed in thought. This caused his father much anxiety since, according to Buddhist mythology, it was prophesied at the time of Siddhartha's

LEFT: The birth scene in Lumbini Grove. This rich narrative painting portrays Buddha's mother who, on her way to her father's palace, suddenly experiences intense pains in Lumbini. As she holds on to the branches of a *sal* tree, her hip seductively thrust out in a pushing motion, she is helped by her elderly maid who presses her waist. Siddhartha emerges from the right side of his mother as a normal baby. He is seen above against the night sky and a mountainous background, with seven steps below his feet. The steps signify his forthcoming fame. Siddhartha takes his first steps in the presence of the great *devas* – Brahma, Vishnu and Siva. This manuscript painting is c. late 18th century, Nepal.

BOTTOM: Head of a young man in stucco, northern India or Afghanistan, 3rd century. The Gandharan style was derived from the numerous influences of various communities engaged in decorating monuments. The young man's gently smiling and friendly face is enhanced with the coloured painting of his head and eyes.

birth that he was destined for greatness, but either as a *chakravartin*, world-ruler, or a spiritual master. A spiritual life, then as now, meant detachment from the conventions of society and worldly pursuits, and like most parents, Suddhodhana was understandably alarmed at the prospect of 'losing' his son.

SIDDHARTHA'S WORLD

The intense young Siddhartha lived in an age not unlike our own. Not only because trade and commerce flourished, but also because there was a questioning attitude towards the dominant religion, Vedic Hinduism. A caste system existed, and its character as a loose organisation of professions in the Rig Vedic period (c. 3000 B. C.), had solidified into a rigid hierarchy that dominated every aspect of life, including one's occupation, who one could or could not marry, and the social relationships one maintained.

Caste also determined one's upbringing, and since Siddhartha belonged to the Kshatriya, the ruler and warrior caste, he was brought

Seen in this Amaravati sculpture, c. 2nd century, is the Buddha-to-be on a prolonged visit to the Tushita Heaven after delivering discourses to the *devatas*. The bodhisattva, in the guise of a white elephant, is ecsconsed in a magnificient palanquin, ready to be miraculously born a prince in the Sakya clan. The scene as described in the *Lalitavistara:* 'A hundred myriad instruments divine and human, gave forth ravishing melody. Hundreds of myriads of *devas*, dwarfs, with willing hands, shoulders and heads bore the grand burden. A hundred thousand *apsaras* led the choirs of music, and proceeding behind, before, in front and on the left and right, praised the bodhisattva with songs of praise. The future Buddha descended as a pure white six-tusked elephant, gilded with gold, and all his members and their parts, his organs without a single imperfection, entered miraculously into the side of his mother Mayadevi.'

up accordingly. This meant acquiring skills related to administration, governance and physical sport, rather than the pursuit of knowledge. With a bright mind inclined towards contemplation, Siddhartha might have found his environment intellectually unsatisfying, especially since the Brahmins took their caste-role as Keepers of Knowledge very seriously and had monopolised scriptural and religious learning by actively excluding non-Brahmins from it.

In this milieu, being a Kshatriya meant, in a way, being spiritually less enfranchised. Young Siddhartha probably felt this keenly, and many years later, as the Buddha, he would denounce the caste system and forbid his sangha, community of seekers, from having anything to do with it. This reform might have come from the caste-related claustrophobia he experienced in his youth, but what seems more likely to have led the Buddha to offer equal spiritual access to all is an understanding of the ultimate interconnectedness and oneness of all beings.

In fact, the caste system and its constrictive influence on the lives of so many was only one symptom of a deeper malaise. Vedic

Hinduism had degenerated into a maze of numerous, intricate rituals that only the Brahmins claimed to know the meaning of. The dominant religion, therefore, had nothing to offer to serious spiritual seekers, who abounded in the India of the sixth century B. C.

This hunger for spiritual experience was growing at a time of immense prosperity. Siddhartha's society was a rich agrarian one. And it was perhaps the abundance of wealth and the consequent good life that prompted many young men to delve into what lay beyond. Prosperity freed minds from survival concerns, thus enabling them to explore and evolve other aspects of their potentiality.

With so many bright young minds engaged in spiritual inquiry, a reaction to the mechanical performance of rituals and blood sacrifices of the Vedic religion was inevitable. In the seventh century B. C. a reform movement began, adopting new paths towards spiritual goals and examining others that had, till then, existed on merely the periphery of religion.

Of all these new streams of thought, perhaps the most radical was that which stemmed from texts called the Upanishads. These texts

Based on Pali literature is this 1st century Gandhara rendition of the child Siddhartha riding to school on a cart drawn by a pair of robust rams. His movement through the streets, together with fellow pupils armed with their *takhtis,* learning boards, and the tree in the background, all add to the setting. As the son of the ruler of Kapilavastu, Siddhartha was provided with all the accoutrements of a 'good life'. He grew up in prosperous times, which were also witnessing a surge towards radical spirituality. This new wave of questioning was engaging the ritualistic Vedic religion in fierce debates.

PAGES 20-21: Pilgrims and monks pray and make votive offerings reflecting the Wheel of Dharma at the Kalachakra ceremony in Bodhgaya. Offerings to Buddha are culturally determined: Tibetans offer yak butter, *tsampa*, barley flour, and scarves; Sri Lankans offer flowers, fruit and lamps.

A decorative crowned Buddha in the Kurkihar style, attributed to the reign of Vigrahapala III, c. 1041-1067. The sculpture depicts the Buddha as a *Chakravartin,* Universal Emperor, or Universal Conqueror of all sin and desire. He sits in the *bhumisparsa mudra,* earth-touching posture, on a lotus. Wearing a three-pointed crown, the *prabha,* aureole, is supported by columns and curves in a cave-like fashion. The trefoil arch is surmounted by the *bodhi* tree and an umbrella.

examined the truth of all existence as being pervaded by the One, known as Brahman, and denied the validity and worship of numerous deities. In addition, the ancient ascetic traditions of *paribbajakas,* literally, seekers, and *samanas*, strivers, were given renewed attention and their meditative practices studied with interest.

By the time Siddhartha was born, this movement had become widespread and powerful and engendered fierce debates and public disputations with practitioners of ritualistic religion. It is possible that these voices impacted and attracted Siddhartha who was then a young prince in Kapilavastu.

THE STEPPING FORWARD

When he was sixteen, Siddhartha was married to Yashodhara, a princess of great beauty.

It is said that he lived a life of indulgence: nights of revelry flowed into days filled with all kinds of pleasures. Perfumed, oiled, clothed in the most expensive silks, Siddhartha sported and hunted, patronised musicians and made love. By material standards, ancient or modern, young Siddhartha had it all.

And then . . . what?

By the time he was twenty-nine, the Sakya prince probably began to wonder whether this was all there was to life. An intelligent person, he began looking around for avenues to sharpen and engage his mind. Some sort of an awakening probably occurred, that brought him to the realisation of the vast and as yet untapped potential that lay within him. Expected to live a nobleman's life, Siddhartha was beginning to acknowledge his own need to move beyond it. Slowly but surely, the time was approaching when he would have no option but to deal with this inner urge.

This was also the point when Siddhartha began considering other issues. For instance, the Four Great Sights that Buddhist scriptures credit with changing the course of his life – that of an old man, a sick man, a corpse and an ascetic – are perhaps meant to be symbolic of Siddhartha's thought process, rather than being taken literally as actual events. It also means that he was looking around with questioning eyes, and along with issues of individual fulfillment, was considering circumstances like death and disease, that characterise the human condition. Perhaps the seeds of compassion were sown at this time; they took root and grew into what was to become the

TOP: Siddhartha prepares for the contest with other princely contemporaries to seek the hand of the gentle Yashodhara. He is surrounded by courtiers who sit gazing in admiration as the young prince gets ready to string a long bow. Siddhartha excelled in archery, horse riding and wrestling. Such narrative sculpture enriched the Amaravati Stupa, c. 2nd century.

BOTTOM: Scenes depicting palace life are the subject of such grey schist stone stupas. The outer railings were surrounded by a *pradakshina- patha* – a path where pilgrims perform the rite of circumambulation. The excellently carved figures, vigorously and sensually designed, and the embellishments were the delight of pilgrims. These dark gray stone schist carvings are rich sources of information on the customs, habits and palace life c. 2nd-3rd century in Afghanistan.

Butter sculpture. After bidding farewell to his sleeping wife and son, Siddhartha cuts his long tresses as a symbol of renunciation of his worldly life. Buddhist monks and acolytes use varied materials to create narrative stories and for decoration. Thick, rich oily butter, conducive to cold climes, is cut into pats of different sizes. It is then carved and coloured. The solidification process is quick. These butter sculptures made by the disciplined, talented youths in the monastery, are used in *thangkas*, paintings, often used to decorate altar tables.

most important aspect of his teachings as the Buddha.

As Siddhartha's mind ripened in contemplation, he felt the need to move on to a life of absolute spiritual commitment. The time had come to renounce his identity as Siddhartha Gautama.

The most rigorous trial of Siddhartha's resolve was the renunciation of his newborn son, Rahula. His silent farewell to his wife and child has engendered many a poignant story and work of art over millennia. Dressed and ready to leave, Siddhartha is drawn to Yashodhara's chamber for a final glimpse of his son. He peeps in, and in the light of flickering oil lamps, sees Yashodhara asleep on a flower-strewn bed, with little Rahula in her arms. A wave of sadness washes over him as he realises that along with wealth and his home, he must renounce them too. Silently, he leaves.

NIRVANA: THE AWAKENING

Cutting off his long hair with his sword and donning the yellow robes of an ascetic, Siddhartha probably inspected the spiritual scene for a teacher. There were plenty to be had. A vibrant *shramana*, ascetic,

tradition had always existed, even if on the margins of Vedic Hinduism. But constant warfare, a higher than ever degree of mass material prosperity, and the questioning of Brahmanical monopoly over religion had perhaps swelled the numbers of those opting out of society to find the truth for themselves.

Siddhartha settled upon Alara Kalama, who had three hundred disciples, as his first teacher, more out of urgency to get started than anything else. He quickly mastered what Kalama had to teach – disciplining the mind to enter the sphere of nothingness. Then, finding that his teacher had nothing else to offer, and that what he had learnt was not the realisation he sought, Siddhartha left.

The meditative methods that Siddhartha learnt from his initial teachers found an echo later in his teachings as the Buddha, in the form of useful tools to help quieten the mind by leading it away from its usual engagements. However, the quietened mind is not necessarily a mind that has understood, or is fulfilled – hence, Siddhartha's need to move on to further discoveries.

Next, he went to Uddaka Ramaputta, from whom he learnt the Upanishadic concept of the one Absolute that manifests in

One of the famous Begram Ivories, the outer cover of a toilet-set box, that were commissioned c. 2nd century by an unknown Kushana prince. Ivory was used for decorative objects or practical use in chairs, table legs, combs and trinkets. Their place of origin may possibly have been Mathura on the trade or pilgrim route. The excavated findings were carefully preserved in the Kabul Museum. These Ivories offered an exciting vista to the mind's eye of palace life during the dynastic rule of the Kushana emperors.

The Great Farewell – 3rd-4th century Gandhara gray schist, Pakistan. In this partially preserved relief, Siddhartha bids farewell to Chandaka, his groom, and his horse, Kanthaka. Having already bid a silent farewell to his family and palace, Siddhartha carries out the final act of renunciation by divesting himself of his ornaments, which Chandaka spreads out his shawl to receive. After this moment captured in the sculpture, Siddhartha would only have to cut off his hair to renounce his nobility. The horse's farewell to his beloved master is movingly portrayed, as he 'licked his feet with his tongue and dropped hot tears', in the words of the 1st century poet, Asvaghosha.
The bodhisattva Vajrapani, believed to be Siddhartha's guardian bodhisattva, stands behind Siddhartha.

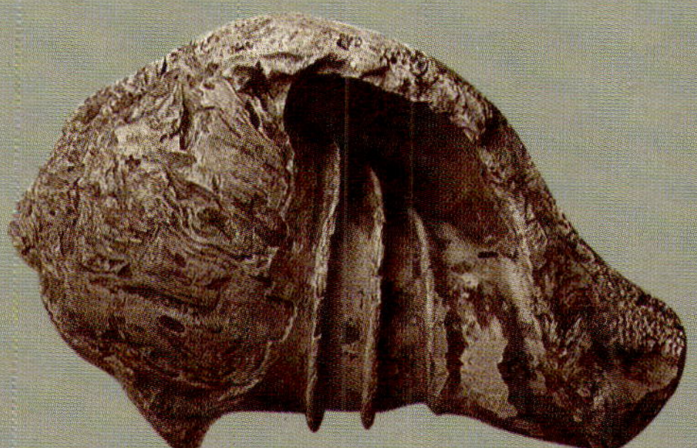

Blowing a conch during rituals is an ancient Hindu practice, something that the Buddhists and Jains seem to have assimilated.
The piercing sound of the conch was used to ward off evil spirits in earlier rites, though in Buddhism the aim was probably a focusing of the mind – a function performed by the gong in Zen ceremonies.

Siddhartha discovers the joy of being
(extract from the Buddha's life)

It is believed that after his six years of harsh penance which did not result in any spiritual fulfillment, the Sakyamuni advocated the avoidance of extreme pain, or pleasure, in his vision of the ideal path for the seeker. This striking sculpture of the emaciated Sakyamuni displays the Gandhara artist's keen knowledge of the human anatomy, seen in the minute detailing of the muscular-skeletal framework of the body. Symbolic of his pre-nirvana state, the ascetic's face has none of the gentle equanimity associated with the Buddha. It is a face tired by exertion, the lips pursed in stern determination.

FACING PAGE: Monks in Paro, Bhutan, unfurl a giant tapestry during the Tsechu celebrations.

This is a story from Gautama Buddha's life. During the years he spent as an ascetic prior to enlightenment, he had become emaciated through prolonged fasting. Driven by an all-consuming desire to know, Siddhartha had withdrawn his consciousness from the physical realm. As a result, his body had begun atrophying. The hair on his body had rotted away and his eyes had sunk into their sockets.

It was in this state that he was meditating under a tree. It was spring and the tree had flowered. A gentle breeze shook a few blossoms from the tree's boughs and wafted them on to the seated figure. The delicate fragrance struck a chord somewhere deep within the ascetic. His mind sought respite from the arduous meditation regimen and turned towards a childhood memory, a path it had assiduously avoided ever since he had renounced his palace and loved ones.

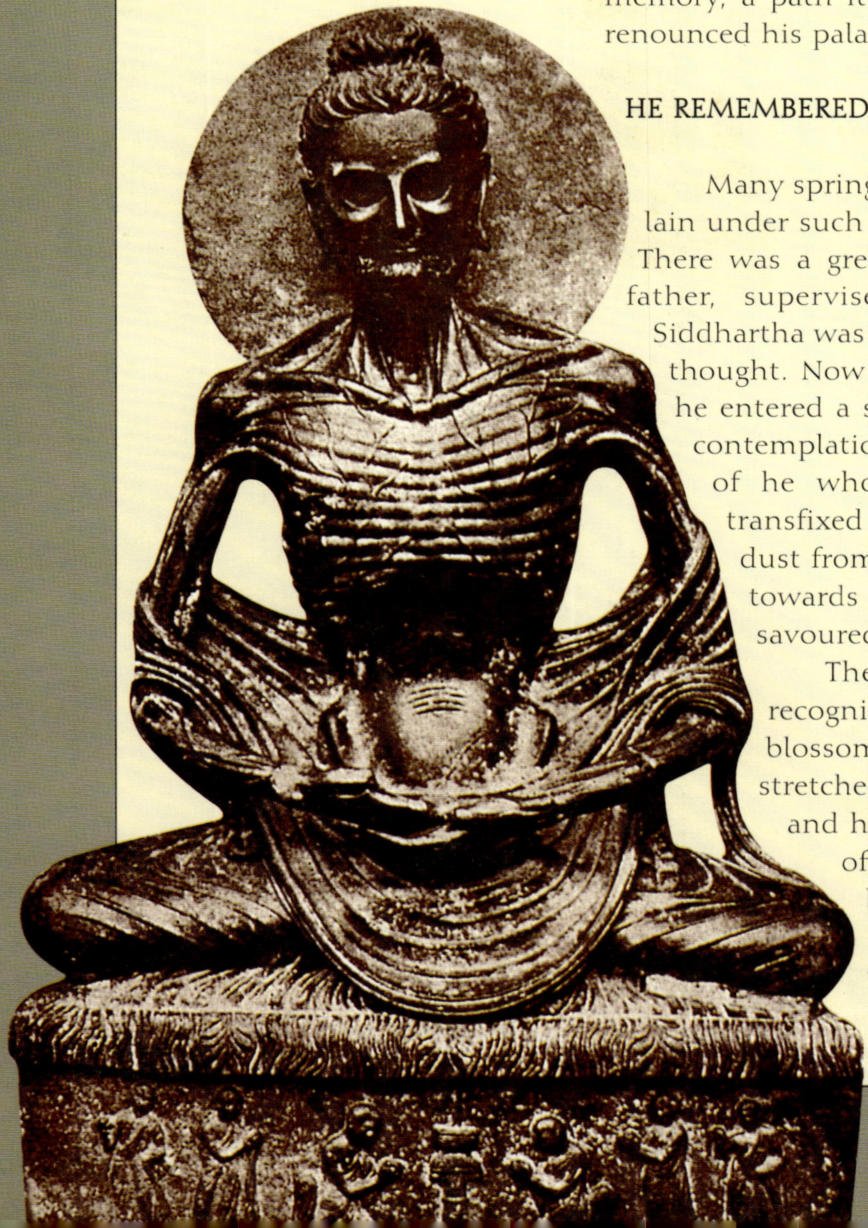

HE REMEMBERED:

Many springs ago, the young prince of the Sakya clan had lain under such a tree, lazily observing the scene before him. There was a great hustle-bustle as Chief Suddhodhana, his father, supervised the harvest. Even then, the young Siddhartha was a pensive child given to long periods spent in thought. Now as he lay enveloped by perfumed blossoms, he entered a state of jouissance, a joy born out of relaxed contemplation. Suddenly, he grew very aware of himself, of he who was observing the scene. He remained transfixed for some time, then brushing off the pollen dust from his jewel-encrusted robes, extended an arm towards a plateful of fruit. The child thoughtfully savoured their juice . . . .

The lean ascetic's eyes opened wide with recognition. The perfume was the same, so were the blossoms. We imagine then that Gautama sat up and stretched his weak limbs. He probably felt his pulse and heard his heart fluttering with the excitement of a new insight. He may have washed his tired limbs in a gurgling stream, and then journeyed on, not yet the Buddha, but glad to be alive!

A scene from Cave III, Ajanta, A. D. 600-642, in which the Prince of Darkness, Mara, sent his daughters to tempt Buddha as he sat in his final meditation towards nirvana. Obviously, Mara is a personification of the inner conflict Buddha faced, and overcame, as he realised the emptiness of all such desires, their direct contact with grasping and, therefore, suffering.

FACING PAGE: The Unseen, Invisible Presence: A pipal tree carving at the entrance to the Sanchi Stupa. The pillars supporting the gateways around the Stupa, are richly carved, notably without any visual representation of the Buddha.
Tree worship, already a feature of the Vedic religion, gained added significance for Buddha's followers following his enlightenment under a pipal tree, later known as the '*bodhi*' tree. The tree was destroyed by an overzealous Hindu king a few centuries after Buddha's death and during the decline of Buddhism in India. Emperor Ashoka's daughter, Sanghamitra, planted a cutting of the original *bodhi* tree in Sri Lanka, where it survives till today.

everything, which he would refute post-nirvana. He also learnt to enter the meditative state that is neither consciousness nor unconsciousness. Yet, this too, was not the fulfillment he sought. Siddhartha left again, and having had enough of teachers, began a rigorous ascetic practice on his own, in the company of five others. Even though he gracefully moved on after learning whatever he could from his teachers, he continued with conventional ascetic practice. Perhaps that was the model available to him and until he reached the ultimate understanding, which could not but be his own, he had to make do with what he had.

For the next six years, Siddhartha remained immersed in deep concentration. It was a harsh, merciless practice. To subjugate his body, he would eat next to nothing, at times restricting himself to one grain of rice a day. Meditating in the forests near the city of Uruvela, in the present-day India state of Bihar, he denied himself protection against the scorching summer and the harsh winter. Soon, he was more dead than alive.

A second century A. D. black stone sculpture from Gandhara,

Sporting a calm, serene smile, this remarkable image of the Buddha, c. 6th-7th century, was discovered in a monastery at Ratnagiri, near Cuttack in Orissa.

FACING PAGE: Skilled Newari craftsmen from Patan (one of the three kingdoms inside the Katmandu valley in Nepal) chisel detail into a rough bronze casting of the bodhisattva Avalokiteshvara, who is probably the most beloved divine figure in Mahayana Buddhism. In the 17th century, Princess Bhrikuti, who married the Tibetan king Tsongsten Gampo, took many Newar Shakya craftsmen to Tibet. It is said that Gampo's marriage to the Buddhist Nepalese princess led to his acceptance of Buddhism.

Pakistan, depicts Siddhartha in this state which was brought on by self-flagellatory penance, his body wasted away, each detail of the skeleton visible under a skin that was no more than a thin film stretched over bones. In the Pali text, *Majjhima Nikaya*, the Buddha recounts: 'My body reached a state of extreme emaciation. My limbs became like the dry and knotted joints of bamboo . . . If I wanted to touch my belly-skin, I encountered my backbone . . . If I rubbed my limbs, the hair, rotted at the roots, came away in my hands'. And at the end of it all, he still had not reached the fulfilment he sought.

Six years into this asceticism, and Siddhartha knew he was doing something wrong. He was no closer to realisation than he had been at the beginning of the practice. With the question, 'Might there not be another way to awakening?' echoing in his mind, Siddhartha ended his severe penance by accepting a bowl of rice from Sujata, a young woman who initially mistook the hollow-eyed ascetic to be a wood spirit. The story is delightful because of the feminine intervention – that and the food are signs of Siddhartha's veering away from ascetic extremes towards a less harsh middle path in his practice.

Even as his companions of six years set their faces against him,

Top: The Mahabodhi Temple at Bodhgaya, first built by Ashoka in the 3rd century B. C. The temple was built at what is believed to be the original site of Buddha's nirvana.

Bottom: A surviving head of the Buddha, c. A. D. 450. The features exhibit the fine craftsmanship of the Golden Age of the Guptas.

Facing page: Cave 19 in Ajanta represents the Mahayana period of Buddhism, wherein the Buddha was personified. Painted in the 5th-6th century, this *chaitya*, prayer hall, displays a standing figure of the Buddha over a tall stupa. The figure is enclosed within an enormous arched doorway. The surrounding columns are topped with capitals. A continuous frieze houses small images of the Buddha in intermittent niches.

Circumambulating the ancient walls of the Tabo monastery dominated by a frieze of Buddhist icons. A woman walks under a row of bodhisattva images, probably praying for their intercession in her problems. In this function, the bodhisattvas are not unlike the Catholic saints that are prayed to, to intercede with God on the devotee's behalf. As there is no God in Buddhism, it is hoped that the bodhisattvas will grant wisdom and courage to sufferers, as well as miraculously effect positive changes in their life – something the Buddha hoped we would learn to do from within, by self-understanding and awareness.

FACING PAGE: A Bon religious dance being performed at the Bonpo monastery in Menri, Solan. Bon religious dances are generally categorised under three distinct themes: morality plays, rites that exorcise demonic forces, and triumphal celebrations of Bon glorifying the deeds of the legendary hero Tonba Sherab.

PAGES 38-39: The *chorten* at Tashiding monastery is regarded as the most sacred in Sikkim. Built by Lama Lhatsun Chenpo, it is believed to contain the relics of the great scholar, Manjushri. Devout pilgrims circumambulate the *chorten*, keeping it on the right as prescribed.

Finishing touches being given to Buddha statues. These are made strictly according to specifications laid out in the scriptures. Measurements and proportions have to be maintained for the image to be consecrated for worship.

BELOW: A cube-shaped tile that separates the first architrave from the second on the south *torana*, gate pinnacle, of the Sanchi Stupa, around the 3rd century A. D. The image of the stupa in the carving is believed to represent the Buddha. The Sanchi Stupa carvings belong to the Hinayana period when the Buddha was not idolised, literally and figuratively, and was represented through symbols such as the lotus, his footprints, and here, the stupa.

FACING PAGE: A conch shell being blown at puja time. Such intricately decorated conch shells are rare, with an elaborate metal covering for the shell and braided silk adorning its far end.

disgusted at what seemed to them a giving up of asceticism, a revived Siddhartha probably washed in the Nilanjana river and sat under a nearby *bodhi* (Ficus Indica) tree.

Till now, he had been striving for realisation; he had been exerting his will. Now, he remembered, from a time in his childhood, an effortless flowing into perfect equanimity. Taking that as his lodestone, Siddhartha felt an ease envelop him. The tightness in his body and mind softened. He vowed that he would not get up till he found what he was seeking.

Six days later, over the four watches of night, it is said that Siddhartha realised his true nature, and that of Reality. In the first watch, he saw all his previous lifetimes. In the second watch, he gained an insight into the birth and rebirth of beings: that this happened due to the nature of their karma, actions, and that this cycle was inherently devoid of substance. In the third watch, he realised dependent origination: that everything exists because of everything else and that by ending ignorance, birth and death can be eliminated. And just before dawn, he saw the Four Noble Truths and the Noble Eightfold Path.

Although the actual nature of what happened is mysterious, we do know that there was a sense of conclusion, and of a supreme connection. When asked for proof of his enlightenment he expressed it through a simple gesture – he touched the earth. That simple gesture conveyed that through his awakening, the Buddha had realised his connection with everything everywhere

Siddhartha, prince of the Sakyas, had ceased to exist. As had the student. And the ascetic.

From under the *bodhi* tree, rose one who had awakened to his true, enlightened nature: The Buddha Sakyamuni, Sage of the Sakyas.

The Jatakas

TOP: The architrave from the north *torana* of the Sanchi Stupa, which is located in the middle of a once well-established caravan trail between Barygaza, a famous Western sea port and Pataliputra, the Mauryan capital. Patronised by Ashoka, its foundation was laid in the 3rd century B. C. Its four *toranas,* gateways, and stone railings are profusely decorated with vivid scenes from the Buddha's life.

ABOVE: A wall painting on clay depicting the Vishvantara Jataka from the Cave of Musicians at Qizil.

Legend has it that Prince Vishvantara once pledged that he would never deny anything to anyone. When, however, he gave away the rainmaking elephant on whom his people were dependent for water, he was banished from his kingdom. Allowed to take only a wagon drawn by four horses, he went with his wife and two children to live in sylvan solitude. After he had given away everything, including his family, the god Shakra appeared in disguise and rewarded him for his generosity.

LEFT: The Jetavana monastery as seen in a roundel from the Bharhut Stupa, Sunga period, 100 B. C. According to the story, a gardener gave Anathapindaka, one of the Buddha's foremost disciples, a large mango fruit. Buddha ate the fruit and instructed Anathapindaka to plant its stone where it would grow. When planted, Buddha washed his hands over it, and a beautiful white mango tree sprang up there immediately. Its branches were loaded with blossoms and fruit. On the right, a man is seen covering the ground with gold pieces and the tree is being watered. On the left, a man is seen tasting the fruit.

TOP RIGHT: The Mahakapi Jataka as depicted in a Bharhut roundel, c. 2nd century B. C. The bodhisattva, in a spirit of extreme sacrifice, was born as a leader of a group of monkeys. He offered his body to be used as a cover to cross the small space that could not be reached by a bamboo bridge, to enable the monkeys to cross over the stream to escape from the king's soldiers who had come to hunt them.

FACING PAGE, RIGHT: Mahajanaka returned to his kingdom, Mithila, which had earlier been usurped by his uncle, Polajanaka. The latter died, leaving one daughter, Sivali, whom Mahajanaka married after fulfilling the conditions laid down by Sivali's father. However, he soon lost interest in his life of luxury and decided to renounce everything and proceed to the Himalayas.

Most wisdom traditions, as they go along, evolve their own mythology in addition to scriptures and philosophical texts. Mythology plays an important part in the religious lives of lay followers. Mythological protagonists are figures central to their belief systems, so it becomes possible to relate to their faith in a space that is non-philosophical and non-didactic. For teachers of the tradition, mythology permits core beliefs to be transmitted in a format that is essentially a stimulus to the imagination, and as such imprints the desired message more firmly in the listener's mind than a dry discourse of dos and don'ts. Mythology might not be true in the sense of being factual; it is more a functional tool of religion.

Since the Buddha's dharma was not confined to renunciates, and perhaps because its lay following at any given time and place was greater than those studying the texts, there naturally came to be a mythology that was uniquely Buddhist. The Jataka tales, five hundred and fifty in all, were an important part of this. These are

BOTTOM RIGHT: A panel illustrating the Miga Jataka set in a medallion on a railing pillar at Bharhut, Sunga period. The bodhisattva was born as the selfless deer that offered his own life to save that of a pregnant doe, to be killed by the king and cooked in the royal kitchen. Moved by this spirit of self-sacrifice, the king gave up killing animals thereafter. This is an important illustration of the Buddhist ideal of ahimsa, non-injury.

stories of the previous lives of the bodhisattva who in his final birth was Siddhartha Gautama, the historical Buddha. Most Jataka stories are based on a particular act of overwhelming compassion by the future Buddha. For instance, in one tale, the bodhisattva, as a monkey, lays down his body across the river Ganga, exposing himself to death so that his companions can escape being caught by hunters. In another, as the Brahmin Sumedho, he humbly spreads his hair before the Buddha Dipankara so that the latter's feet do not get soiled as he walks. Other tales provide examples of acts of self-sacrifice of the bodhisattva in the form of diverse creatures, from rabbits to tigers and goats.

Most Jataka tales are based on pre-Buddhist stories and are interesting in the way they afford a glimpse into the times of the Buddha. Like animal fables in Greek, native North American and the Inuit cultures, the Jataka tales have a moral content informed by Buddhist virtues. Over the centuries, they have been told, retold and carved repeatedly on stupas and temple walls throughout the Buddhist world.

Bottom left: Cross-bar medallions appear in decorative abundance. The lotus flower in all its natural beauty makes for an opulent floral motif. It lends an exquisite disposition as a background to personages. In the middle of the flower is a fair maiden, holding a bunch of flowers. This is a typical Bharhut medallion, c. 2nd century B. C.

The Yava-Majhakiya-Jataka relates vividly how an innocent maiden foiled the evil intentions of the well-placed male friends of her absentee husband. So intent were they on outraging her modesty that they unwittingly fell into her trap. She summoned them one by one at hourly intervals to her abode in the dead of the night. Persuading them to bathe, her handmaidens then proceeded to oil their bodies with soot, and concealed them in baskets. The villains are seen here humiliated, the fourth still tied up in a basket in the foreground. The sculptor's rendering of the king on his throne, disbursing justice, reveals how, in Bharhut sculpture, noble and upright males protected and cared for a maiden in distress.

LEFT: A portion of a pillar sculpture on which is inscribed in Brahmi – *Suvanna Karkataka.* A *karkataka*, crab, and other creatures can be seen scuttling around with an eye to appeasing their appetite. Many Jataka stories tell of the machinations of greed and cunning. Such pieces of sculpture were removed by noblemen and refitted into new locations. This piece is one of the few that has survived, though not in its original form, and is now preserved in the National Museum.

RIGHT: Part of the Prasenjit pillar. Trees were used as a symbol of the 'invisible Buddha' in Bharhut images. They not only had botanical value but also served as pictorial representations, surrounded by Buddhist symbols. The feeling of awe they invoked served to lend an inner certainty to the presence of the Buddha, hidden, and yet present.

THE ESSENCE OF BUDDHA'S DHARMA

For some time after his awakening, the Buddha remained silent, perhaps meditating on his insights. Then, seven weeks later, he made his way to the Deer Park at Sarnath, near the modern-day city of Varanasi, where he met his five former ascetic companions. He spoke to them for the first time about his realisation. With this, according to Buddhist scriptures, the Buddha set the Wheel of Dharma in motion.

BASIC TEACHINGS

Part of that first sermon at Sarnath consisted of the Four Noble Truths. These pithy statements are said to contain the distilled essence of the Buddha's understanding of the human condition. Akin to all his discourses throughout his life, they were spoken in Pali, the language of the masses, instead of Sanskrit, the language of the learned, and displayed the Buddha's propensity for saying things as directly as possible, side-stepping the verbosity and sophistry that were the hallmarks of religious discourse.

The First Noble Truth is the recognition of the inherent dissatisfaction with life. And this is not something to avoid thinking of but to recognise it for what it is. What causes it? According to the Second Noble Truth, it is desire, or more appropriately, craving that causes dissatisfaction. The more we crave for and grasp at pleasure and try and run away from unpleasantness, the more dissatisfied we are likely to be. Accordingly, the Third Noble Truth says that a wholeness of being can be achieved through cessation of craving and grasping. But how? By following the Eightfold Path: the answer lies in the Fourth Noble Truth.

The Eightfold Path can be considered to be the Buddha's advice for right living. It includes having the right view, right resolve, right speech, right action, right livelihood, right effort, right mindfulness and right

TOP: (SEE PAGE 13.)

BELOW: Votive stupa, c. 9th century, Nalanda. During the Pala reign, Buddhist monasteries were notable for promoting stone and metal sculpture. This tall votive stupa is square based, with eight panels showing different scenes from the Buddha's life. The view shown in this image portrays the attainment of nirvana. The Buddha lies on his right side, his right arm holding a cushion under his head as a support, and one leg over the other. He delivers his last sermon to his disciples. Eight Avalokiteshvaras, two on either side, are visible on the pedestal.

FACING PAGE: A row of brass Buddhas seated in dignified splendour. Brass became popular much later for making images of the Buddha.

A close-up of an architrave decorating the north *torana* of the Sanchi Stupa, c. 1st century. The circular design in the foreground, moving in one direction, is complimented by a garden on the side, with fruit-bearing plants and birds enjoying themselves. The gardener hovers behind, shooing them away. The double-storey gateway is graced by maidens carrying water pots. The scene depicts an episode of the Vessantara Jataka. Since the stupas were meant to be circumambulated, putting the artwork on the gates allowed them to be easily viewed and comtemplated upon as the followers made their round of the stupa.

TOP: One of Leh's numerous Buddhist monuments.

Above: This little-known stupa, 100 B. C., was excavated in a village called Keshnapalli in Andhra Pradesh. The *Chandrasila,* half-moon, shaped stone, marks the four points of the ambulatory path around. Marked on the base line is *Sri,* good fortune, from which emerges a spray of young lotus flowers. This stupa is a *damura,* donation stone. The names of Ayupu Deva of the Thera sect and his disciple Aya Badhaka are associated with it.

Facing page: The Buddha's eyes gaze from the Swayambhunath Temple in Nepal. Believed to be the oldest stupa in the world, even prior to its construction, people circumambulated the hill in worship. Both Buddhists and Hindus worship here.

concentration. While it has become common to use 'right' while describing the elements of the Eightfold Path in English, the Pali word used by the Buddha was *samma,* which translates better as 'balanced'. So in effect, what the Buddha was asking us to do was to bring various aspects of life in harmony with one another. This can be done by living in awareness, in a state in which every act is done consciously and therefore, 'rightly'.

THE MIDDLE WAY

The Eightfold Path to balanced living emanates from the very heart of the attitude that has come to be known as Buddhism's Middle-Way approach to spiritual seeking and indeed, to life. The germ of this probably came from the Buddha's own experience of two extremes – his indulgence in pleasure as a young nobleman, and in self-inflicted hardship as an ascetic.

He is quoted in the Pali text *Samyutta Nikaya*: 'Giving oneself up to indulgence in sensual pleasure: this is base, common, vulgar, unholy, unprofitable. Giving oneself up to self-torment: this is painful, unholy and unprofitable. Both these extremes the Perfected One has avoided, having found that it is the Middle Way which causes one to see and to know, and which leads to peace, to knowledge, to enlightenment.'

Walking the middle path, then, means spending every moment in awareness, with an open, at-ease mind. Pain and pleasure, laughter and

tears, labour and rest – all are to be imbued with the quality of mindfulness. Actions are to be skilful, expressive of a mind anchored in equanimity, brought about in turn by meditation.

INTERDEPENDENT ORIGINATION

One of the most original of the Buddha's insights is perhaps that of *pratitya samutpada*, conditioned origination. According to this belief, everything is interdependent on everything else. Death occurs due to birth; birth takes place due to becoming. Buddhist scriptures go on to trace a long chain of causation with numerous linkages. The becoming is said to be conditioned by grasping, which rises from craving; craving, in turn, comes from feeling, which is due to a sense-contact, which arises from the physical body. The physical body arises from cognition, the cause of which is impulse, which we experience because of our ignorance.

The reason why *pratitya samutpada* is interesting is because it affords an insight into the Buddha's approach to the human situation. Further, it is based on analytical step-by-step reasoning that was not divinely divulged or psychically communicated. It was achieved by a calm, purified mind; but a human one, nevertheless.

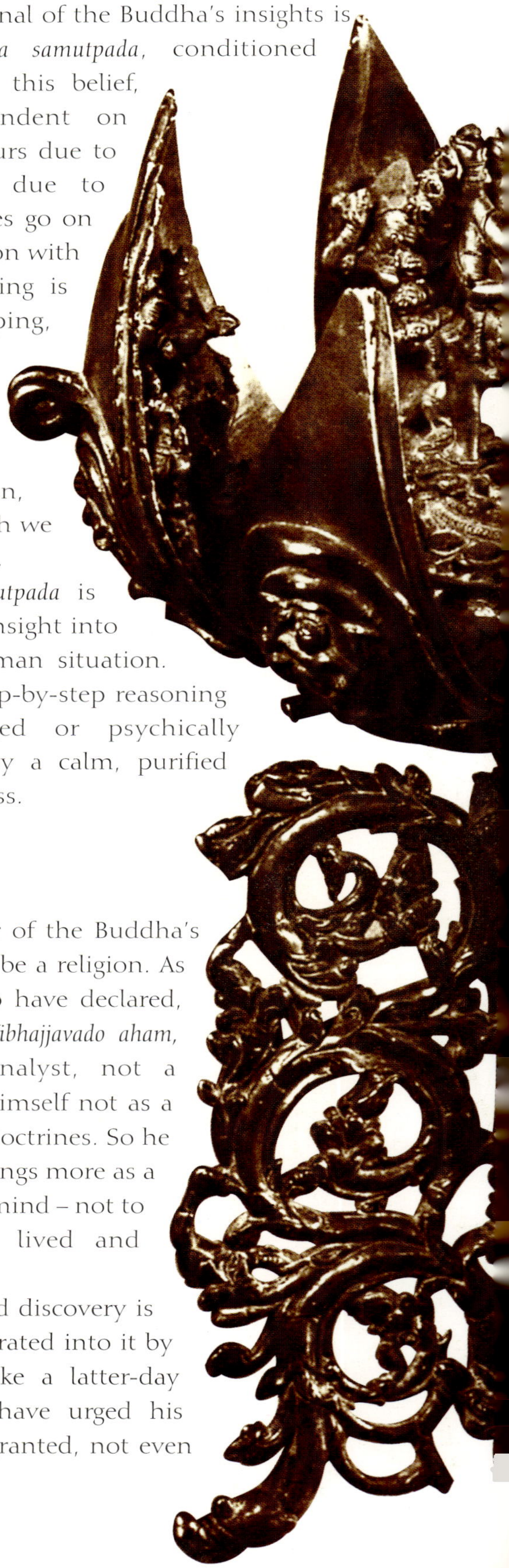

SELF-EFFORT AND DISCOVERY

This brings us to the character of the Buddha's Way. It was definitely not meant to be a religion. As the Buddha himself is supposed to have declared, and the *Majjhima Nikaya* quotes: '*Vibhajjavado aham, naham ekamsavado*! – I am an analyst, not a doctrinaire'. He clearly positioned himself not as a propounder, but as a questioner of doctrines. So he would have seen his path and teachings more as a theory of existence, a science of the mind – not to be blindly followed, but to be lived and experienced.

This emphasis on self-effort and discovery is integral to Buddhism and was integrated into it by the Buddha himself. Somewhat like a latter-day scientist, the Buddha is said to have urged his followers not to take anything for granted, not even

ABOVE: Buddha *Pada*. The footprints relate to the Buddha's crossing of the river Nairanjana, near Bodhgaya. In the wheel the *tri-ratna* symbol represents the three jewels of Buddhism: the Buddha, the dharma and the sangha. They lie below the *dharmacakra,* the Wheel of law. The toes are imprinted with the swastika. Buddha's foorprints symbolised him and his path.

TOP: This small roundel is one of a large hoard of semi-precious, mostly silver miniature objects discovered in the Oxis river in 1887. It is an exquisite repousse medallion of an elephant, probably transporting the Buddha's relics. Stylistically, this belongs to the Gandhara School, Kushana period, c. 1st century.

what he said. They were to verify each statement and doctrine for themselves, by living it, and questioning it Clarifying the importance of individual striving, and also his relationship with his followers, the Buddha says in the *Dhammapada:* 'You yourself should make the exertion. The *Tathagatas*, Buddhas, are only teachers'.

In fact, this was the very last thing that the Sakyamuni had to say to his followers. As he lay dying, his foremost disciple, Ananda, asked him for a final teaching. 'Be a lamp unto yourselves,' said the Buddha, and fell silent to embrace his approaching death. This, like so many others, appears to be a jewel of understanding, gleaned from his own experience. He had followed teachers, and learned from them, but true realisation had come when he sat under the *bodhi* tree and became a lamp unto himself.

NO GOD, NO SELF

According to Buddhist scriptures, whenever the Buddha was asked about his view of God, he remained silent. It is likely that the Buddha believed such a Supreme Being to be non-existent and non-real. Yet his silence was probably meant to convey that he did not wish to get involved in debates on a subject that had little or no direct relevance to his endeavour to help individuals seek greater clarity and understanding about themselves and their lives. Especially since a large chunk of the theological debate at the time was centred on this very issue and Brahmins, Vedantins, *lokayatas* or materialists, and Jains, who were atheists, spent a lot of time and energy stating their points of view and presenting counterpoints. The Buddha seems to have wished to distance himself from all this hair-splitting, since he probably did not think it was an issue real enough to be addressed, and so left it open through neither acceptance nor denial.

However he appears to have been more vocal about the atman, or the individual self. Vedantic thought from the Upanishads spoke of the atman as an individual portion of the Eternal One, the Brahman. As thread in a necklace, it was believed to run through successive rebirths until all karmic fruits were exhausted and the atman could merge back into its source, the Brahman. The Buddha overturned this doctrine on its head and spoke instead about *anatta (anatma* in Sanskrit), which meant 'Not Self'

The Sanchi Stupa abounds with flourishes of fauna and animal life. The brilliant peacock often seen on the surfaces of railings and pillars, strides around fanning his tail of vivid colour. The depiction of animals is probably due to the influence of the Jatakas, which showcase the Buddha as various animals in previous lifetimes.

PAGES 52-53, CENTRE: A lotus mandala, Bengal, 11th century, brass with paint, symbolises the merger of tantric ideas and practices with Buddhism, leading to the rise of Vajrayana, the Thunderbolt Vehicle. At the centre of the mandala, stand Hevajra and his consort Nairatmaya in deep embrace, surrounded by eight *dakinis,* feminine energies. They try to rouse Hevajra, for it is through his awakening that one's true nature (Buddhanature) can be achieved. The outer part of each petal has two tiers of reliefs. Each lower register displays a snake, stupa, fire, tree and two figures, one of whom is dancing. Each upper register depicts two figures – the *Mahasiddhas,* perfected beings.

Monks and their acolytes, as part of their contact with the lay population, and in accordance with the sangha's routine, give up all earthly possessions and, during the monsoons, retire to their monasteries in splendid isolation. Every morning they go on their rounds with a simple begging bowl and receive helpings of rice and cooked vegetables. The bowls are decorated with a simple design, enabling their identification.

This rare sculptural creation from Sarnath depicts Avalokiteshvara, the bodhisattva of compassion. Also known as Padmapani, the lotus-bearer, he is identified by a minute representation of Amitabha above his forehead. The elegance and grace of the face are typical of Gupta art, c. 5th century.

FACING PAGE: Wooden masks elaborate the monastic tradition of celebration and reveal the mystical aspects of the Buddhist pantheon. Balanced precariously and tied only with cords on the youthful head of a lama, the carved mask, facing all directions, depicts the all-seeking philosophy. The masks take on the characteristics of the monastery where they produced by the monks themselves.

Lamas at prayer.

BOTTOM: Crossbar from a railing, Bharhut, Madhya Pradesh, c. 2nd century B. C. Made in red sandstone, the man's face emerges from within a lotus medallion enclosed with a string of pearls. It could be a celestial being adoring the Buddha, or the donor of the railing. Giving donations to temples and monasteries has always been considered a way of earning a better future birth. This is further borne out by the inscription that reads: *Mitasa suchi danam* – This crossbar is a gift of a friend.

FACING PAGE: The Abbot of Punakha bestows his blessings on the faithful.

PAGES 58-59: Bodhisattvas made in brass. Bangkok is said to have over 400 *wats*, Buddhist temples, adorned with beautiful Buddhist artwork.

PAGES 60-61: The Je Khenpo, Chief Abbot of Bhutan, keeps watch over the Punakha Dromche as masked dancers keep evil spirits at bay.

According to the Buddha, nothing, absolutely nothing, is permanent – not Brahman, not the universe, certainly not any individual self. Belief in the permanence of anything was to him the greatest ignorance of the nature of reality, which he saw as essentially *sunya*, empty.

He did speak of rebirth, though, which might seem impossible without a transmigratory soul. But, explained the Buddha, it was not an atman that flowed through consecutive births, but rather a set of *skandha*, characteristics, that appeared in each birth. The self was really as insubstantial as everything else and with this recognition, the characteristics that the self had assumed fell away, and nirvana was actually achieved.

What really is nirvana? Is it a Buddhist version of the Judeo-Christian reward in afterlife, or like the Vedantic moksha – a post-death exodus towards an omnipresent Oversoul? Nothing so esoteric, it seems. Nirvana does not appear to have been laid out by the Buddha as something 'out there', that one inched towards in a linear progression. So although the concept of the *parinirvana* or post-death nirvana does exist, nirvana by and large seems as simple as a freeing of the mind from fundamental ignorance. It was an extinguishing, not in the literal sense, of the self, but a rooting out of the ignorance that led to grasping and so to suffering. At the core of the Buddha's teachings is the movement from the suffering of ignorance to the nirvana of knowing.

The Dalai Lama on Compassion

A well-known fresco from Cave 17 at Ajanta Caves, Maharashtra. The Buddha's appearance is enhanced by his size which dominates that of the mother and child, said to resemble Yashodhara and Rahula. Perhaps it is an iconic representation of Rahula kneeling with folded hands, asking for his inheritance. The Buddha's gesture with his begging bowl suggests that he is without any possessions. An emotional scene, the facial expressions of the mother and child are poignant with adoration and humility.

BOTTOM RIGHT: The Kanishka reliquary, casket, of the Emperor Kanishka, once containing the emperor's relics, from Shahji-ki-Dheri. Cast in a heavy bronze composition in the Kushana style, c. 1st century A. D. It is now preserved in the Peshawar Museum in Pakistan. Discovered by Spooner in 1908 at the stupa close to Peshawar, the site was verified by Hiuen Tsang, the Chinese Buddhist pilgrim. The lower part of the reliquary has an image of the King.

In Tibet we say that many illnesses can be cured by the one medicine of love and compassion. These qualities are the ultimate source of human happiness, and our need for them lies at the very core of our being. Unfortunately, love and compassion have been omitted from too many spheres of social interaction for too long. Usually confined to family and home, their practice in public life is considered impractical, even naive. This is tragic. In my view, the practice of compassion is not a symptom of unrealistic idealism but the most effective way to pursue the best interests of others as well as our own.

The foundation for the development of good relations with one another consists of altruism, compassion and forgiveness. These bring humanity together so that no conflict, however serious, will go beyond the bounds of what is truly human. A mind committed to compassion is like an overflowing reservoir – a constant source of energy, determination and kindness. Or this mind can be likened to a seed: when cultivated, it gives rise to many other qualities, such as tolerance, inner strength, and the confidence to overcome fear and insecurity. The compassionate mind is also like an elixir: it is capable of transforming bad situations into beneficial ones. Therefore, we should not limit our expressions of love and compassion to our family and friends. Also compassion is not only the responsibility of the clergy or health-care or social workers. It is the necessary business of every part of the human community.

As long as we live in this world, we are bound to encounter problems. If, at such times, we lose hope and become discouraged, we diminish our ability to face difficulties. If, on the other hand, we remember that it is not just ourselves, but everyone who has to undergo suffering, this more realistic perspective will increase our determination and capacity to overcome troubles. Indeed, with this attitude, each new obstacle can be seen as yet another valuable opportunity to improve our mind. Thus we can strive gradually to become more compassionate, by developing genuine sympathy for others' suffering and the will to help

remove their pain. As a result, our own serenity and inner strength will increase.

The need for love lies at the very foundation of human existence. It results from the profound interdependence we all share with one another. However capable and skilful an individual may be, left alone, he or she will not survive. To me it is clear: a genuine sense of responsibility can result only when we develop compassion. It is because our own human existence is so dependent on the help of others that our need for love lies at the very foundation of our existence. Therefore we need to develop a genuine sense of responsibility and a sincere concern for the welfare of others.

PAGES 62-63, CENTRE: The lotus in full bloom – a symbol of the Buddha. Very few roundel-medallion shaped stone pieces from Amaravati, c. 2nd century A. D. remain. Far removed from its origins, this relief madallion is preserved in the British Museum.

BOTTOM: The Dalai Lama addresses monks of his order, the Gelug. His Holiness wears many hats – the yellow one of the lineage holder of the Gelug sect being one of them. He is today an enduring symbol of compassion and has helped interpret the Buddha's path in a modern context.

PAGE 64: A young monk supports the ceremonial pipes, while two others blow into them. These pipes are part of many Tibetan Buddhist ceremonies.

THE MOVEMENT FORWARD

SECTS AND THE SANGHA

The Buddhist sangha, community of seekers, emerged with the first sermon at Sarnath, where the Buddha accepted his five former ascetic companions as his followers. For the next forty-nine years until his death, the Buddha roamed the country, walking through cities and villages, stopping often to discourse and converse. Wherever he went, many men, and later women too, accepted his teachings, some as lay followers, others as *bhikkus*, monks, and *bhikkunis*, nuns.

TOP: (See page 13.)
BOTTOM RIGHT: Whosoever this mottled sandstone, headless, feetless and armless Kushana sculpture, c. early 2nd century A. D. represents, noteworthy are the proportionate dimensions of the diaphanously clad semi-nude male figure. The waist cloth is coiled and wrapped around the front and tied at the side and rear. A simple multi-strung necklace adorns the neck.

THE REFUGE

In the beginning, there appeared to have been no formal initiation into the sangha. The aspirant's commitment and the Buddha's assent, non-verbal at times, were thought to be sufficient. As was customary among ascetics of the time, the *bhikku* would then shave his head as a symbol of his renunciation and simply follow the Buddha, in his journeys and in his teachings.

As the sangha grew rapidly, the Buddha encouraged his monks to ordain, thereby enabling the sangha to grow organically and develop a life of its own. He did outline an elementary ceremony though, in which the initiate was to seek refuge in the Three Jewels: Buddha, dharma and sangha by repeating three times:

Buddham sharanam gacchhami
Dhammam sharanam gacchhami
Sangham sharanam gacchhami.

I take refuge in the Buddha
I take refuge in the *Dhamma* (Pali for Dharma)
I take refuge in the Sangha.

The Buddhist Trinity: the Buddha in the centre; the bodhisattva Avalokiteshvara on his left, identified by the image of Amitabha in his crown; the bodhisattva Maitreya, messiah yet to come, on his right. Emerging from the deeply sheltered background are Brahma and Indra, seen wearing a tall crown. Gandharan sculpture exhibits a profound fusion of blissful sensuousness and spirituality. The Buddha's form expresses vitality and well-being, while his smile exudes benevolence. Seated in *padmasana,* his fingers are entwined in *dharmacakra mudra.*

Given his own possible experience of Brahmanical rituals as a Kshatriya nobleman, where the means had become ends in themselves and tended to lead away from the metaphysical core, it might have occurred to the Buddha that this ritual-like ceremony was not really necessary for spiritual engagement. Yet he was perhaps also aware of man's basic need to lend a framework to his actions, which is what ritual does. And a new monk probably needed the reassurance. Apart from this concession, primary Buddhism seems to have had no ritual.

A SOCIAL VISION

Initially, when the sangha was still more like a band of followers, the Buddha would journey with them all the year round, except during the monsoon when torrential rains forced them to seek shelter in caves and later, in *viharas*, retreats. For a few months every year, wandering came to a halt. It is likely that this time was used for introspection.

With the expansion of the sangha and the building of monasteries by wealthy patrons and kings, some monks were allowed to live settled lives. These settlements were usually on the periphery of towns, and not far away in forests. One reason might have been that the Buddha did not wish his sangha to exist in isolation. Rather, he envisaged a social duty for his *bhikkus*.

A Buddhist *bhikku* is not a monk in a Christian, or even an Indian *shramana* sense. The Buddha probably saw him as a sharesman: one who received a share. His begging for alms was symbolic of his renunciation of possessions and therefore of his reliance on common wealth. In that sense, the *bhikku* was very much a part of society and often had a symbiotic relationship with patron householders, with whom he shared his *dhamma* and knowledge, and offered a spiritual perspective on worldly matters.

This integration of the sangha and society appears to have been a first in India, where earlier on, spiritual seekers had wandered out of society. The Buddha led them right back in, thereby giving the sangha an integral vision that was really another articulation of the middle path, which took into account both social responsibility and spiritual seeking.

SANGHA DEMOCRACY

Rulers who embraced the Buddha's *dhamma*, like the powerful Bimbisara of Magadha and Pasenadi of Kosala, among

Illustrated palm leaf manuscripts accompanied by text often portray important events in the Buddha's life. The four main texts are the *Mahavista*, the *Nidanakatha*, the *Buddhacharita* and the *Lalitavistara*. The above is from a well-preserved palm leaf from the Asiatic Society Library, Kolkata.

BELOW: Head of a bodhisattva from the Gandhara period, late 2nd century. The bodhisattva is a spiritual saint, endowed with his own purity and serene beauty. Every minute detail is wrought with perfection. The curly hair arranged in a chignon is decorated with strings of pearls interlinked with metal buckles. Just below the chignon are visible the damaged remains of either the *triratna* or the *srivasta* symbol.

FACING PAGE: Theravadin Buddhist monks stroll through the forest grounds at Siaminika Monastery, Sri Lanka. For Theravada Buddhists, the path to nirvana is an individual pursuit achieved by practising monastic discipline and meditating on the impermanent nature of reality.

RIGHT: The Miracle of Walking over the Water: a narrative sculpture from the Sanchi Stupa East Gate, c. 1st century. Battling against a ferocious storm, are ducks and men in a boat riding on waves. Each tree crafted with meticulous detail, makes this pillar a masterpiece. The trees in the middle segment are clearly mango trees. Below them are pipal trees with long, pointed leaves inscribed in Pali as *Bhagavata Saka Munino Bodi* – the Holy Pipal of the Sakyamuni.

BOTTOM: A terracotta representation of a monk, Gandhara period, c. 3rd century. A clean-shaven skull with a forehead creased and wrinkled, the stern look is aggravated by the two deep lines around the mouth. Images of Buddhist monks appear more often in groups but when seen individually, the poise and dignity they depict, reveal the status they were accorded in society.

PAGES 72-73: The Ladakh Festival. Dances in colourful costumes form the mainstay of festival celebrations. However, Ladakhi dances have not gained popularity outside Ladakh since the region has remained largely cut off from the rest of the country till recently. Most costumes belong to the local *gompa,* monastery, and are kept in the temple of the protective deities.

others, granted their sanghas amnesty from the laws of their lands. Thus it fell upon the Buddha to ensure that all the members of his sangha behaved appropriately and that the kings' exemption was not misused. For, we must remember, that the vast sangha included people from all castes and social classes who were not used to living in such close proximity with one another. Even though they were following the Buddha's teachings, it is likely that tensions arose and the scriptures do indeed record instances where quarrels broke out among monks even during the Buddha's lifetime.

It is interesting to note that the Buddha seems to have regulated the sangha along the lines of a republic. Perhaps this was an echo of the years he spent in the Sakyan republic. In the sangha republic, the Buddha's position was equivalent to that of a ruler by virtue of being the founder. Next to him were his chief disciples Sariputta and Moggallana, who owed their position to spiritual merit. In due course, a leadership group developed comprising monks senior in ordination and those who were said to have attained the status of *arahants*, conquerors of afflictive emotions. Any monk or novitiate could voice his opinion when important decisions were taken by the entire assembly. There was no vote, however, and the matter was discussed until everybody reached a consensus, indicated by silence.

The sculptor's vision of the daily life of the people – their dress, tasks and their preoccupations. In this pictorial representation, the perfectionist's hand is manifested in the inventive way he uses a single dimension, by placing people, animals and architectural structures one above the other, formulating almost three-dimensional levels. There is a pervasive innermost sensation of feeling emanating from the manner in which the flora and fauna relate to their surroundings – the trees imbuing a warmth and glow that shows how wonderful life on earth was then.

BELOW: Isi-Singiya-Jataka, Bharhut, 2nd century B. C. ' When the great bodhisattva was born as a Brahman, he withdrew to the forests of the Himalayan region, perfecting his knowledge and his piety. By some miracle a doe gave birth to a human boy whom the ascetics in the region raised as Isi Singa. He grew up, became a recluse, learned and pious. With these gifts he became very meritorious.' The medallion – a bas relief – reproduced here depicts only the first part of the story: the bodhisattva living in a simple style in the typical manner of hermits in the forest. The story continues on another medallion, that strangely, has not so far been found.

PAGES 74-75: Monks with cymbals at the Rumtek Monastery in Sikkim. This monastery was established by the 16th Gyalwa Karmapa, head of the Karma Kagyu sect, as his seat after he fled Tibet subsequent to Chinese occupation. The high lama's successor is appointed by an unusual reincarnation process. Today, however, as Rumtek awaits the 16th Karmapa's successor, the issue is mired in controversy with two rivals claiming the seat. Though Ugyen Trinley Dorje, the young lama who fled Tibet and arrived in Dharamsala in early 2000, has received the Dalai Lama's approval as the 17th Karmapa, he is yet to be formally enthroned at Rumtek.

Apart from the basic sangha rules pertaining to non-violence, non-possession, celibacy and eating before noon, most others were subject to change. The greatly detailed dos and don'ts especially for women, which we now see in Buddhism, were probably codified well after the Buddha. For during his lifetime, he appears to have always searched for the middle path in this matter as in all others. For instance, once in the middle of a discourse, he sneezed and his discourse was interrupted by someone blessing him. The Buddha forbade such blessings or responses to them. On realising, however, that this was considered rude by the townspeople, he allowed the practice. This example, although seemingly a small one, illustrates the openness of mind that the Buddha brought to everything.

CHANGE AND SCHISM

Adoration of the Buddha's alms bowl, an Amaravati cross-bar roundel, 2nd-3rd century, added during the renovation of the stupa by Nagarjuna. It portrays the Buddha's alms bowl being transported to heaven. The flying *apsaras* bear garlands and the huge tray is held aloft for all to see and gain merit. Over fifty celebrants are seen in joyous conglomeration, glorifying the moment. People gaze in adoration as they are overwhelmed with spiritual upliftment.

BELOW: A bronze sculpture, with inlays of copper and silver, of Lokeswara, the bodhisattva known as the Lord of the World. This highly formalised representation, c. 12th century A. D., Sena dynasty, Bengal, depicts the Buddha more like a god-like being.

The Buddha passed away in 483 B. C. at the age of eighty, in Kushinagar. Fearing that the order would disintegrate, senior monks decided to meet during the first rainy season after his death to try and canonise the Buddha's teachings and his discipline, called *vinaya*, for the sangha. At this meeting, referred to by Buddhist scriptures as the First Council, the *bhikku* Upali was asked to lay down the rules for the sangha, and the *bhikku* Ananda, the Buddha's teachings. Others were free to interject if they remembered anything other than what was stated. By the end of this meeting, a canon had been established and committed to memory.

Significantly, Ananda, who had for long been the Buddha's attendant, mentioned the Master's having said that some minor rules of the *vinaya* were subject to change, or could be abolished altogether. Immediately Mahakassapa, who seems to have been much concerned about the 'correct' preservation of everything, asked Ananda what these rules were. When Ananda admitted that he had not actually asked the Buddha, the Council decided not to take any heed of his statement and preserve all the rules as they were.

So what was preserved for posterity at the time was, in effect, the monks' perceptions of the Master and his wisdom. At times, these could have resulted in the recording of what the monks thought the Master had said, or what 'they' felt should be. Moreover the writing of the teachings didn't start until two centuries later. So we must remember that what has been written as 'the Buddha's words' may not be exactly so; it may contain many extrapolations and modifications. It is also believed that in order to lend greater credence to the phenomenon of nirvana, which was increasingly presented as the goal of every Buddhist, his realisations were sought to be presented as having occurred in one flash of enlightenment.

The ensuing century wrought many more changes in the character of the sangha, and in the path itself. As often happened in India, with the passage of time, the memory of Buddha Sakyamuni, the man, grew dim, and was replaced in the mass psyche with a divine saviour-like figure. Images of him began to be made, the earliest in the manner of the Greek god Apollo, and worshipped. Alongside sprang the cult of bodhisattva worship, bodhisattvas being believed to be possessors of great powers which they used to help other beings. And so, it would appear, many Buddhists were back to square one: worshipping deities and asking for wish fulfillment.

Even as these changes were radically altering the fabric of the Buddha's path, which was fast acquiring characteristics of a theistic religion, there was a part of the sangha that persisted in preserving the original teachings as they were. The Second Council, held a hundred years after the first one, brought the schism out in the open. Thereafter two schools of Buddhism came to be recognised – Mahayana, which embraced change, and Theravada, literally, Supporters of the Doctrine of the Elders.

In what might seem to be a case of one-upmanship, Mahayana followers began to refer to Theravada practices as Hinayana, the Lesser Vehicle, thereby setting it up in opposition to Mahayana, the Greater Vehicle.

With its entry into Tibet several centuries later, Buddhism acquired a third *yana* – Tantrayana. Going by the names alone might give one a sense of progression – from lesser to greater to a seeming acme, with a notion of the latest being the best, not unlike latest models of vehicles of a different kind!

This might be a view believed and propagated by followers even today. But what seems more likely is that each *yana* is a different way of traversing the same path – trundling along diverse by-lanes and dirt tracks, but empowered with the same essential ideas. The notion of there being as many paths to realisation as there are seekers, is a time-honoured tradition of Indian spirituality. The Buddhist *yanas* seem to be an extension of the same idea, offering a palette of practices to seekers. Much more than being just schisms, we can attempt to see them as an expression of the variety of seekers that were led to Buddha's path.

Even though most of the Buddha's figure is missing in the remains of this Gandhara style sculpture, 1st-2nd century, it is striking because of the two overawed ascetics crouching before the Buddha. Their emaciated bodies portray the austerities that they have subjected themselves to. Wearing a loin cloth and sporting matted hair and beards, they look towards the Buddha with adoration and thirst for knowledge. This could be a depiction of the Buddha's first sermon a few weeks after his awakening, at the Deer Park in Sarnath near Benares. The ascetics could be two of the Buddha's five companions to whom he spoke for the first time about his realisation. This sermon is known as the *dharmachakkapavattana* – Setting the Wheel of Dharma in Motion.

PAGE 78: A bedecked image of the Jowo Sakyamuni at the Jokhang Temple in Lhasa, Tibet.

NAGARJUNA:
Founder of Madhyamika

Nagarjuna (A. D. 200-300) was an Indian Buddhist philosopher who founded the Madhyamika School of Mahayana Buddhism. He studied both the secular and religious branches of Hindu knowledge before turning to Buddhism and spent most of his life in the great Mahayana centres of learning in south-east India. Two texts most clearly present his views: the *Mulamadhyamikakarika* (Stanzas of the Middle Way) and the *Vigrahavyavartani* (Treatise on Averting Arguments). The former is read and studied by philosophers of all major Buddhist schools of Tibet, China, Japan and Korea and is one of the most influential works in the history of Indian philosophy. Nagarjuna's stature in the Mahayana and Vajrayana traditions is enormous and the Tibetan tradition even identifies him as a magician-alchemist.

The Madhyamika School is characterised by its logical refutation and negation of all philosophical systems, Buddhist and non-Buddhist alike, while claiming no unique philosophy of its own. Nagarjuna's philosophical method is referred to as negative dialectics. He especially attacked the *Adhidharmas*, claiming that the real agenda of dharma theory, atomism, was not really momentarism, time or causality but a new form of *anatta,* substantialism. It is an unfolding argument culminating in the triumphant assertion of the reality of only emptiness. Despite lacking any essence, he argues, phenomena exist conventionally, and conventional existence and ultimate emptiness are in fact the same thing. This represents the radical understanding of the Buddhist doctrine of the two truths, or two levels of reality.

Nagarjuna tries to re-establish the Buddha's middle path, affirming neither existence nor non-existence, permanence nor impermanence, identity nor difference, but showing the relativity of all conceptions. Even the basic elements of dharma, existence, are taken to be void of ultimate reality.

The bodhisattva Avalokiteshvara, a sculpture originated from Kurkihar, during the reign of Ramapala, 11th-12th century. He sits on a double lotus in *lalitasana;* his right foot rests on a lotus emanating from the base, suggesting that a *prabhamandala* was in place on another base. His right hand is stretched out, bestowing blessings and boons. The left hand holds a lotus stem which blooms over his left shoulder. Wearing a girdle with pearls around his waist, the other jewels comprise a necklace, bracelets, arm-bands and a beaded sacred thread that drapes over his right thigh. Notable are the twin *kirtimukha,* faces, on his arm-bands. His hair, arranged in a coiffure on top of his head, contains an effigy of Amitabha.

An angry Buddha.

FACING PAGE: A detail of the bodhisattva Padmapani (see page 92).

PAGES 80-81: Tibetans, lay and monk, celebrate Losar, their new year, by throwing *tsampa,* barley flour, in the air. The revelry is probably accompanied with shouts of *lha Gyallo,* Victory to the Gods. Losar is a time of celebration and making offerings for a bountiful year. Tibetans in national dress gather on the third day of Losar at the stupa to burn juniper branches for purification. There is a huge prayer ceremony led by a high lama, where grains of rice are thrown in the air as offerings during the prayers. At the end of the ceremony, *tsampa* is thrown in the air for good luck, showering all in a blanket of white. People gather to sing traditional songs and dance in praise of the Dalai Lama. New songs speak of the day of freedom when the sun will shine through the clouds on their great land.

พระพุทธสันติทีปนฒถ

NEW HORIZONS

If one travels from one end of India to the other, along ancient highways and once-mighty cities, one is likely to come upon pillars and rocks a couple of millennia old, inscribed with exhortations to follow the Buddha's *dhamma*. Written in long-forgotten dialects and scripts of the third century B. C., these rock edicts are remains of the first, and perhaps the only, Buddhist state in India.

RULE BY *DHAMMA*

Though there were royal followers even during the Buddha's lifetime, none attempted to rule by the *dhamma* as did Ashoka. He was the king of Magadha, the north-eastern state where the Buddha is believed to have spent much of his life. Ashoka expanded his empire through conquests, so that it extended from the borders of Persia to modern Goa in the south, and to the Ganga's delta in today's Bangladesh.

Ashoka belonged to a monarchy that had, three generations earlier, been inducted in a statecraft that was fundamentally amoral and required great deviousness and cunning on the part of the ruler. It had been devised by Kautilya, who went on to evolve a definitive treatise on similar lines, called the *Arthasastra*. According to the treatise the primary duty of a ruler was to expand the boundaries of his empire by any and all means. Ashoka followed this initially, as had his father and grandfather, until the Kalinga War took place.

It is said that Ashoka waged a particularly brutal and bloody war against the Kalinga republic, which lay south of his kingdom in the modern Indian state of Orissa. On winning the war, he rode out jubilantly, only to find corpses everywhere. The horror of the sight ultimately made him turn towards the Buddha's *dhamma*, not only as his personal religion, but also more importantly, as state policy.

TOP: (SEE PAGE 13.)
BOTTOM: Dharmapala, the protector of dharma, Tibet, c. mid-18th century. Dharma is depicted here in its highest connotation: to perform one's duty for its own sake. It also implies justice, virtue, righteousness, law, religious merit, the good, the true, the normal and the ideal. Here, Dharampala embraces his sakti energy in the form of his female consort. He stands in *alidhasana*, with both feet trampling the back of a recumbent creature. In his two hands he holds a wand and a skullcap. He wears a garland of skulls, cast in bronze, with traces of gilt.
FACING PAGE: A splendid aspect of the Buddha glitters in the the bright Thai sunlight, in Koh, Samui Beach.

A bas-relief in a roundel from Amaravati in Andhra Pradesh, 2nd century. This roundel is comparable to an act of terrorism, wherein a cowardly man, concerned only about his own safety, projects the imminent danger on to an innocent stand-in. Devadutta, Siddhartha's jealous cousin, with the intent of killing Gautama Buddha, poisoned the gentle elephant's meal, resulting in the animal losing control and becoming violent and dangerous. Nalagiri entered Rajgir, Buddha's rain retreat, and ran amok in an uncontrollable rage. He is seen here holding a terror-struck victim, upside down in his trunk. Panic-stricken women watch the attack from the sidelines. The next scene shows Nalagiri kneeling down before the Buddha, perhaps calmed by his compassion that extends to all sentient beings, not only humankind.

Ashoka became an ethical Buddhist ruler, attempting to embody the *dhamma* in every aspect of governance. His version of the *dhamma* was that of a layman, rather than of a monk, and was largely devoid of philosophical content. It was concerned only with moral and ethical issues. For instance, the opening sentence of his Second Pillar Edict says: 'Thus speaks Devanampiya, the king Piyadassi (Ashoka): *Dhamma* is good. And what is *dhamma*? It is having few faults and many good deeds, mercy, charity, truthfulness, purity, gentleness and virtue.'

The king never fought a war again, and devoted himself to the cause of building a *dhamma*-based administrative machinery. This meant an active integration of the Eightfold Path and primary Buddhist values of non-violence and generosity into policy-making and organisation. Resources of the state were used for public welfare. Animals, too, were treated with compassion. Not only was hunting discouraged, but 'medical services provided (for them) along with human beings', informs the second Major Rock Edict.

Even though the Buddhist state collapsed after Ashoka's death, the reverberations of his unique experiment are felt in India till today. The Wheel

TOP: A masterly copper-cast sculpture, c. early 19th century, with traces of gilt in the Tibet-Nepalese style. The Buddha is seated in *vajrasana* on a lotus base mounted with large petals. Noteworthy is the realistic manner in which his *samghata*, robe, is draped across his body from his left shoulder in a flowing manner to rest on his right forearm. His right hand is in the *varada mudra*, and his left elegantly placed on his lap.

RIGHT: Part of a casing stone for a stupa at Gummididurru in Andhra Pradesh, this fragment is rendered in the delicate Amaravati style. Seated under the *jambu* tree, Siddhartha thought about the miseries of existence. He talked to a monk about it and the latter advised him to renounce the world. Placing the fragment showing the departure above the miracle of the *jambu* tree, is thus appropriate.

FACING PAGE: A composite palace scene, Amaravati, c. 150-225 A. D. The prince, seated on a couch, looks down at an entertainer who holds aloft a tray on which a wriggling snake is poised. The court ladies add a touch of glamour.

of *Dhamma*, used by Ashoka in his state symbols, to indicate a synergy between spiritual values and temporal rule, has been inducted in the flag of the modern Indian republic. The spirit of Ashoka's tolerance, which accepted 'diversity in unity', had a profound effect on Mahatma Gandhi, the twentieth-century apostle of peace. Gandhi would comment that his view of secularism was similar to that which prompted Ashoka to declare: 'One should honour another man's faith ... concord is to be commended so that men may hear one another's principles.'

Dhamma Travels

Even though his warring days were over, Ashoka's interest in the unknown and the unreachable remained. It urged him to embark upon conquests of a different kind: conquests of peace, love and *dhamma*. Ashoka sent bands of *bhikkus* to distant lands to scatter the seeds of the Buddha's teachings as far and wide as they could. It is because of those efforts that today, the Buddha's words continue to echo in various parts of south and south-east Asia, many centuries after they fell silent in the land of his origin.

The island of Sri Lanka was where the *dhamma* was first sent; it took root instantly, much like the cutting from the original *bodhi* tree, taken and planted there by Ashoka's daughter, Sanghamitra. Ashoka's son, the *bhikku* Mahinda, is said to have initiated the king, Devanampiya Tissa, and others into Theravada Buddhism. When asked whether the 'establishment of Buddhism' in Sri Lanka had been successful, he replied: 'When a son born of Sri Lankan parents, becomes a monk in Sri Lanka, studies the *vinaya* in Pali and recites it in Sri Lanka, then the roots of the *dhamma* would have gone deep'.

Buddha-*sasana*, rule by dharma, in the spirit of the Ashokan experiment in India, was thus established in Sri Lanka. So much so that the long line of Sinhala kings who ruled the island until the British annexed it in 1815, were not only Buddhist, but also bodhisattvas, a homegrown Buddhist version of the medieval European monarch's Divine Right to rule. Unbroken state patronage in Sri Lanka ensured the survival of Theravada Buddhism, and of its canon, which had disappeared in India but exists in its entirety in Sri Lanka, having been transcribed in Pali, c. 43 B. C.

In later centuries, Sri Lanka acted as a nerve centre from which Buddhism pulsated forth to south-east Asia. This was especially so in the twelfth century, when a Theravada revival occurred under the dharma king Parakkramabahu. Much in the manner of Ashoka, he sent out missions by

MANDALA: COSMIC DIAGRAM

A mandala is a ritual diagram that serves as an object of meditation in tantra and Vajrayana Buddhism. It is symbolic of the universe. Around the eleventh century, mandala meditation was introduced in Tibet from India and even today, lamas pass on their knowledge to initiates in the same way. Mandalas are constructed at the beginning of a puja, out of grains of coloured sand carefully placed on a specially prepared platform. They are temporary structures and in a teaching of impermanence, are deliberately destroyed at the end of the ritual, their sand swept up and poured into a nearby stream or river.

The word Mandala is derived from the root *manda,* essence; and *la,* container. Thus, a mandala is a container of essence. As an image, it may symbolise both the mind and the body of the Buddha. The origin of the mandala is the centre, the *bindu,* a dot – a symbol free of dimensions. *Bindu* also means seed, sperm or drop – the salient starting point. It is the gathering centre into which outside energies are drawn, and in the act of drawing in the forces, the devotee's own energies unfold. In the process, the mandala is consecrated to a deity.

In its creation, a line materialises out of a dot. Other lines are drawn until they intersect, creating triangular geometrical patterns. The circle drawn around stands for the dynamic consciousness of the initiated. The outlying square symbolises the physical world bound in four directions, and represented by the four gates; and the central area is the deity. The centre being visualised as the essence, and the circumference, as grasping, a mandala thus signifies a grasping of the essence.

All monks in Tibetan Buddhist monasteries are required to learn how to construct mandalas. They have to memorise texts that specify names, lengths and positions of the primary lines defining the basic structure of mandalas, as well as the techniques of drawing and pouring sand. These texts, however, do not describe every detail of each mandala, but rather serve as mnemonic guides to the complete forms that must be learned from the repeated practice of construction under the guidance of experienced monks.

Monks carefully constructing a mandala, mystical diagram, with coloured sand. As is evident, the making of a mandala is a tedious process, requiring great concentration and attention to every intricate detail of colour, line and form. Once the ritualistic purpose is over, the sand is swept away – one more teaching in the impermanence of things.

FACING PAGE: A Buddha figure in a Tibetan temple, with a mandala on the roof overhead. The figure of the Buddha can be seen in the centre of the mandala, which might be supposed to exemplify the being of the Buddha and his nirvana. Contemplation of such a mandala would be intended to help the practitioner grasp the essence of his own Buddhanature by following the diagram of spiritual experience laid out in the mandala.

A *thankha* from Thimpu in Bhutan. Painted in an artistic style typical of the region, it is an aspect of Avalokiteshvara, early 20th century. The somewhat stylised seated figure shows the arms normal with hands folded in the *anjalihasta,* salutation, whilst the additional arms are raised, and the lotus blossom is seen only on the left side. The background comprises nature's luscious foliage.

BOTTOM: Bodhisattva Padmapani, sculptured in a typical stele, in gray-black schist, Pala dynasty, c. 8th-11th century. Five Buddhas sit at the apex of the carved figure seated in *lalitasana* on a double lotus, with a lotus blossom on either side.

sea routes. The first bastion to be established was in Burma (now Myanmar), where the Sinhala monks converted the king and obtained royal patronage. Thailand followed a century later under a similar royal diktat, while Cambodia and Laos adopted Theravada Buddhism in the fourteenth century.

ALONG THE SILK ROUTE

In the course of its extensive spread, Buddhism found itself traversing all possible paths and lands. Between Ashoka's rule in the third century B. C. and c. 50 B. C., it found its way into west and central Asia through the ancient Silk Route. We can picture caravans loaded with bales of silk and brocade from the palaces of Peking and the bazaars of Varanasi being joined by barefoot monks on preaching missions. Along with treasured spices, *Buddhadharma* wafted through post-Alexandrian Gandhara into central Asian desert-oasis towns. Here, Mahayana monks preached to populations of Afghans, Turks and Mongols.

From Grotto 1 at the Ajanta caves in Maharashtra is this vision in mural, painted in colour, c. 6th century. Modelled with an extraordinary finesse, almost asserting a diaphanous flush to the bare flesh, his face is lit up with an expression of spirituality. The genius and virtuosity of the Ajanta painters was orchestrated by the resident monks whose knowledgeable guidance inspired the actual accomplishment of the murals. Grotto 1 is awash with paintings of the highest quality.

Tathagata Akshobhya, a transcendental Buddha, c. 10th century, heavy bronze-copper alloy with traces of gilt. Behind is his emblem – the *vajra*. Devotees of 'Vajrayana's teachings' were inclined perhaps towards the increasing attraction of tantrism, followed by Asanga and Nagarjuna who expounded upon topics such as *srishti*, creation; *pralaya*, dissolution; *sadhana*, spiritual exercises; *dhyana*, meditation, and rituals relating to magic. Extant literature c. 7th-8th century upto 12th-17th century is mostly untranslated. Thousands of manuscripts were destroyed, including the *vajravanic* text. This is a calm and introspective sculpture of a classiv yogic asana. The surrounding aureole of tongues of leaping flames accentuate the world of marvels in contrast to the serenity underlying the transcendental tathagata's personae.

This frontier outpost of Buddhism was only highlighted in the last century, when shrines and monasteries were discovered in the Taklamakan desert by the scholar Sir Aurel Stein. That this Silk Route Buddhism was Mahayana is evident from the figures of the Buddha, like the recently destroyed Bamiyan Buddhas, and manuscripts of Mahayana scriptures rendered in ancient central Asian languages.

LIGHT OF ASIA

Around A. D. 50, the dharma travelled along the Silk Route in the other direction as well, towards China. There, it was faced with the ancient Chinese philosophies of Taoism and Confucianism. While the latter dealt mainly with ethics and social conventions, the former was a simple but enigmatic philosophy based on direct experience of the essence of life, or absolute

reality. Buddhism was initially regarded with some degree of suspicion, being referred to as the alien 'Wisdom from the West'. Then, as Indian monks began translating Buddhist texts into Chinese dialects, words with Taoist connotations would often be used to explain Buddhist concepts. This made Buddhism more acceptable to the Chinese. For instance, dharma came to mean *Tao*, The Way, and nirvana became *Wu-wei*, Non-action.

In the sixth century A. D., an Indian monk, Bodhidharma, arrived in China. He introduced the centrality of dhyana, meditation, into Chinese Buddhism. A fervent meditator, Bodhidharma is believed to have sat for nine years staring at a wall before agreeing to teach. Even though the Buddha's path was essentially one of contemplation, its Chinese avatars were either wholly devotional in nature or were based on the study of particular texts, such as the *Lotus* or *Garland Sutras*. Bodhidharma swung the needle back to introspective sitting meditation, which went on to evolve into yet another sect of Buddhism known as Ch'an in China and later as Zen in Japan.

FACING PAGE, TOP: Ancient tantric rituals being performed at the Tabo Monastery in Spiti.

FACING PAGE, BOTTOM: Lamas in Black Hats and masks lead a procession to exorcise evil spirits. Elaborate costumes, masks and headgear are used for a ritual dance.

BOTTOM: Seated in *rajalilasana*, Simhananda Avalokiteshvara rides his ferocious lion with an air of regality like a king. The sculpture is in the Pala-Bengal style, c. 16th century. Other influences are apparent in the projection of the lion.

DHAMMA IN FLUX

As the *dhamma* braved uncharted waters and inhospitable terrain abroad, its very nature was undergoing radical change in India. Even though with hindsight, we tend to view and talk of it as Buddhism, giving the impression of a monolith evolving and moving from one stage to another, the Buddha's *dhamma* has really always been a dynamic entity. Its sects not only co-existed with each other and with the several varied spiritual paths and philosophies of the time, but drew liberally from one another as well. This wondrous flexibility, the ability to undergo several mouldings without losing its intrinsic character, stood Buddhism in good stead, whether in Brahmanical battles in India or during survival pangs elsewhere. In a way, this also resulted in the roaring river of wisdom that Buddhism was in its heyday, quietening into a gentle stream that fed the multi-watered ocean of Indian spirituality.

Dhamma could be embodied as state policy, as happened in the Ashokan era. However, due to its emphasis on balanced living, it seems to have never replaced popular religion in the life of the masses. For most of its life in India, Buddhism probably remained an urban phenomenon, and the sangha was confined to cities and townships. In the villages, it could never really displace Vedic gods and goddesses, rituals and worship, and soon, the Buddha was inducted into an ever-burgeoning divine pantheon as an avatar of the deity Vishnu. Also, Buddhism did not have a centralised church or clergy and even though royal patronage enabled its widespread adherence, at the end of the day, the householder needed a socio-religious

The all-seeing eyes of the supreme Buddha stare out in each cardinal direction from the gilded spire of the stupa at Swayambhunath Temple in Nepal. The four directions are at times held to indicate the Four Noble Truths. The red spiral question mark denotes dharma – the path to self-awareness. Skilled Newari artisans carved miniature stupas and Buddha statues around the courtyard at Swyambhunath. Devotees make flower offerings and apply coloured powder to the figures.

FACING PAGE:
A beautiful rendering of Tara, the feminine embodiment of compassion, Katmandu, Nepal. With the evolution of Vajrayana, which has its roots in tantra that worships the Divine Feminine, women acquired greater acceptance and importance than they had previously in Buddhism. Indeed, each Vajrayana bodhisattva and deity has a female counterpart, and some female bodhisattvas, like Tara, became independently popular.

PAGES 98-99:
Pemayangtse is the principal monastery of the Nyingma sect of Tibetan Buddhism. An incomparable repository of religious art, it was built by Chador Namgyal in the early 18th century. Here, monks unfurl an appliquéd *thangka,* scroll, on the monastery façade during the annual Chaam Festival.

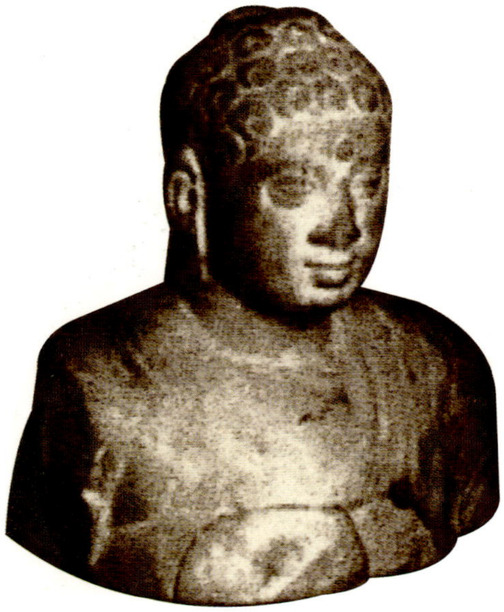

TOP: A bust of Lord Buddha discovered in the late 1920s at Nagarjunakonda. This site came into being c. 225-236 A. D. It is believed that Nagarjuna spent his last days in a monastery Sri-Parvata, later renamed after him.

A piece from a casement slab, probably with a series of dhyana Buddhas sitting in a row. The Buddha is seated in an interesting variation – the lotus flower with its well-defined petals is used to enhance the position of the Buddha, who is seated on a stool. His hands are placed in the gesture of dhyana.

structure within which to conduct his life. Birth, marriage and death - indeed, all rites of passage had to be commemorated. Priests were needed, not just monks.

To fulfil these needs, Buddhism appears to have appropriated existing customs and traditions wherever it went. In India, this happened in the form of a growing dependence on Hinduism, and the incorporation of its practices, as in the case with tantra. In Tibet, deities and rituals of the existing Bon shamanism, were given a place in Buddhism, and in China, there was a happy merger with Taoist philosophy. Friendly inclusion, rather than fierce exclusion, was practised, in keeping with the *dhamma's* universal spirit.

THE TANTRIC VEHICLE

In India, this spirit of inclusion, spurred in part by survival urgencies, is what is believed to have spawned an eminently successful experiment of Mahayana Buddhism with tantra. The emergence of brave new creeds like Buddhism and Jainism had put the ancient Vedic religion, with its nature-worship and sacrifices, in decline, leaving a void. However, Indian ingenuity with spirituality led to the growth of several paths, one of which was tantra. In preceding centuries, tantra had arisen almost as a life-affirming response to the austerities practised by ascetic cults. Its recognition of the spiritual and material as being inextricably interlinked in man was perhaps one of the most radical ideas in the history of Hinduism. By the seventh and eighth centuries, tantric practices and philosophy were coming into their own and making an impact in mainstream religion.

Faced with the growing popularity of Hindu tantra, Indian Buddhism resorted to its ace survival tactic – If you can't beat 'em, join 'em! Tantric rituals, beliefs and techniques of symbolism were incorporated, but not before being primed for Buddhist tastebuds with a dash of *sunyata* and a sprinkling of noble truths. Tantrayana became the new vehicle on the block and came to be regarded as the 'express train' to nirvana. For, instead of the causal, step-by-step teachings of the other *yanas,* Tantrayana helped one leapfrog, in one go, beyond the mundane by using the power of one's imagination.

The root of this lies in tantra's acknowledgement of the sacredness of all life and phenomena. Nothing is evil or repulsive. In the Buddhist context, this translates into a view of the First Noble Truth of suffering as mental conditions, happy or otherwise, arising from and subsiding in an essentially changeless Buddhanature. Thus desires, too, are not to be identified with or repulsed, but are viewed as energy that can be positively transformed into the altruistic energy of compassion and loving kindness.

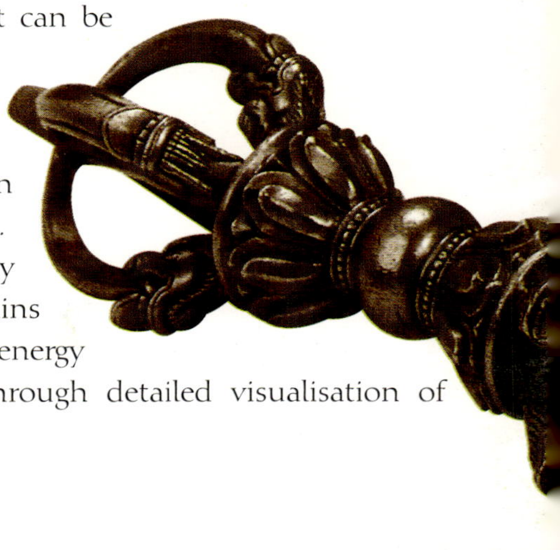

According to Tantrayana, human beings exist as gross and subtle bodies. Made of vital energy, the subtle body operates with the gross body and contains within it the energy system of cakras, energy centres, and *nadis*, energy channels. Through detailed visualisation of deities such as the bodhisattvas Avalokiteshvara, Maitreya, Tara, and so on, the practitioner is supposed to work on his energy body, and acquire the attributes of the deity. By leaping into a direct perception of one's inherent Buddhanature, the limited self has been transcended and an understanding achieved. Tantrayana is, however, only fantasy if not practised in awareness of the kernel of *sunyata,* the emptiness of all phenomena.

The fascinating deities of Tantrayana, which were later immortalised in Tibetan Buddhism, were creative manifestations of both human and Buddha-like attributes. Those like Avalokiteshvara and Tara are formalisations of compassion. Such symbolism, a very tantric characteristic, is also seen, for instance in the replacement of the five Buddhist aggregates of human personality with the five Buddhas: Vairocana, ethics; Amoghasiddhi, freedom; Ratnasambhava, concentration; Amitabha, appreciation; and Akshobhaya, consciousness. This symbolism was also important for a lay disciple, for the concept of five Buddhas inhabiting his body was infinitely easier to accept than dry concepts, and helped to focus his attention on a higher goal.

THE TIBETAN THUNDERBOLT

By the middle of the seventh century, Indian Buddhism had embarked upon what in time would prove to be its greatest and most significant journey. Not only would it help preserve its teachings in their entirety and genuineness thirteen centuries into the future, it would in a time far ahead, help shape a worldwide Buddhist renaissance.

Into the vast silences of the Tibetan plateau, inhabited by the shamanistic Bon religion, the Buddha's *dhamma* was introduced during the reign of King Srongbtsan by his two Buddhist wives, one from China and the other from Nepal. Between themselves, the two managed to convert the king. Thereafter, a long line of scholars and monks from the Indian monastic universities of Nalanda, Takshashila and Vikramashila wended their way into the forbidding land of snows, carrying with them the scriptures and practices of almost all the prevalent sects and streams of Buddhism.

The first among these was Padmasambhava, revered by Tibetans as Guru Rinpoche; he helped establish a predominantly Tantrayana form of Buddhism, which mingled with the local culture, and elements of Bon came to be woven into it. Tibetan Buddhism ultimately came to be called Vajrayana, the thunderbolt vehicle to nirvana. This, of course, was the result of constant innovation and exchange between Indian and Tibetan masters over the next few centuries.

TOP: The figure's posture suggests that he is a Mahasiddhar Virubba. His right arm is raised in the gesture of instruction and his right hand holds a *vajra.* In his left hand he holds a precious jewel. Seated, a *yogapatta* tied around his right leg secures him. Skulls in his headgear decorate the rim. This Tibetan gilted bronze sculpture is c. early 18th century. The five tathagatas are seen in his crown. He holds the bell and the *vajra,* thunderbolt.

PAGES 100-101, BOTTOM CENTRE: The ritual bell cast in bell metal, decorated with Buddhist symbols, gives a resounding ring when tapped on the circular ring top. The *vajra,* thunderbolt, is a weapon, held by Indra, and Vajrapani.

BELOW: An elegantly coiffured Vajrasattva, Kashmir, 8th century, brass with silver inlay. Seated in *lalitasana* on a lotus, above uneven rocks, two nagas sit in adoration below him.

'OM MANI PADME HUM'

TOP AND BOTTOM: The great Tibetan mantra, *Om mani padme hum,* engraved on metal (top) and rock (bottom). It is also often printed on prayer flags and written on slips of paper and stuffed into the heart of a prayer wheel, so that with every flutter of each one of the flags and every turn of the prayer wheel, the vibrations of the mantra are sent out into the atmosphere. The intention might be to create a positive force field around oneself and one's community, and of course, to gain merit.

The great mantra of Tibetan Vajrayana is *Om mani padme hum.* Inscribed on prayer wheels that are kept constantly turning and on multi-coloured prayer flags that flutter benedictions in all directions, this mantra is central to the Tibetan way of life. Although the words mean Hail the Jewel in the Lotus, the mantra is believed to have significance beyond the literal. At one level, the jewel and the lotus can be seen as the dharma and the Buddha. At the tantric level, the mantra denotes the intercourse of the Buddha with his feminine sakti, or Avalokiteshvara with Tara. While *mani* and *padme* share a grammatical relationship, *om* and *hum* are syllables that cannot be easily translated.

At a purely syllabic level, the six syllables of the mantra have been interpreted as corresponding with the six *paramita,* perfections, of the bodhisattva. These are generosity, patience, meditation, morality, energy and wisdom. Somehow, the mantra has also got engaged with the idea of accumulating merit in the form of good karma, and part of the energetic turning of prayer wheels and the constant chanting with prayer beads is geared towards the end of notching up as many *Om mani padme hums* as possible. This repetition is an important part of the Tibetan laity's life of dharma. Centuries of being regulated to suit diverse human breathing and speaking patterns has rounded the edges of the mantra, so that it no longer has the clear-cut edges of the original Sanskrit, and has settled more or less in the comfortable groove of being *Om Mani Peme Hung.*

Vajra literally means Thunderbolt, and Vajrayana, rooted in Tantrayana, was the vehicle that cleared misconceptions clouding one's Buddhanature through radical shifts in consciousness. It became possible within a shorter length of time, to achieve a direct experience of reality through tantric practices that helped drop the distorted self and its perceptions, rather than spending a lifetime overcoming them. Desire too was pressed into service, and detachment from grasping and attachment, was actually to be cultivated in its positive avatar of compassion for all sentient beings. Even today, this Vajrayana effect is evident in the life of the Tibetan people, who despite innumerable hardships, are able to smile through it all.

In Tibet a dharma rule was established in a more complete way than the Ashokan state had ever been. Not only was a new alphabet developed from Sanskrit to enable easier translation of scriptures, political power ultimately passed into monastic lineages of bodhisattva rulers in the thirteenth century. In a unique albeit feudal experiment, temporal power was identified with spiritual prowess and the right to rule passed to the head of the Sakyapa lineage in A. D. 1244. By the fifteenth century, it had passed on to the Gelugpa School, and the Dalai Lamas have ruled Tibet since then. In the last century, the country was annexed by China and the Dalai Lama had to flee to India, where there continues to be a Tibetan government-in-exile.

Today Buddhism continues to move into new territory, carrying with it the Buddha's teachings of wholeness and compassion wherever it goes.

TOP LEFT & RIGHT: Buddhist mantras, yantras and mandalas were commonly depicted in *thangkas*. A recently painted *thangka* (left) portrays a magical mandala in brilliant colours, the subject being protection to ward off any intrusion. The guardian king (right) of a cardinal region, possibly in the west, holds a stupa in his left hand.

BOTTOM: A typical Nepalese classical bronze hollow cast decorative head of the Buddha, 60-70 years old, for the personal adoration of devotees.

PAGES 104-105: The Boudhnath is a prominent monument in Nepal, and the atmosphere around resounds with the chants and turning of the prayer wheel rising into the redolent air.

Padmasambhava: Guru Rinpoche

TOP LEFT: Chatral Senge Dorje Rinpoche seated on a tiger skin in Yanglesho, Nepal. He is considered to be the greatest living master of Dzogchen – the highest and subtlest of Tibetan Buddhist teachings, 'The Great Perfection', the apogee of Tibetan Buddhist meditative accomplishment. It is believed that Dzogchen cannot be taught or learned – either you get it or you don't. Chatral Rinpoche resides most of the year in the 'hidden land' of Yolmo Kangri.

TOP RIGHT: Yangsi Urgyen Rinpoche during his enthronement. It is believed that the Rinpoche carries with him many lifetimes of learning that will be shared in this lifetime with his followers. Born in June 1993 as the youngest child of Chokling Rinpoche, he is the reincarnation of Dilgo Khyentse Rinpoche. Yangsi Rinpoche was enthroned at Shechen Tennyi Dargyeling Monastery, in Boudhnath on 5 December, 1997.

BOTTOM: A Buddhist stupa at the entrance to a village in central Nepal.

FACING PAGE, TOP: Taktshang Monastery, Tiger's Nest, is so named because Guru Rinpoche is said to have flown to the site on the back of a tigress. He then meditated in the cave for three months.

FACING PAGE, BOTTOM: In the Swat Valley, Pakistan, a Buddhist Gandhara stone sculpture of Guru Rinpoche with his two consorts, Yeshe Tsogyal and Mondrova.

Padmasambhava, whom the Tibetans revere as Guru Rinpoche, was an eighth century tantric adept from India who helped establish Vajrayana in Tibet. A century before his arrival, c. A. D. 779, Buddhism had been introduced in Tibet during the reign of King Srong-btsan. Even though Buddhism received state patronage from Srong-btsan and his successors, possibly because they saw it as an escape route from the power of Bon priests, it was yet to displace Bon as the faith of the people. In this sense, the arrival of Padmasambhava marked a turn in the fate of Buddhism in Tibet.

The pantheistic Bon religion that Padmasambhava encountered was the ancient faith of Tibet, dominated by belief in and worship of deities and spirits. As a practitioner of Tantrayana, Padmasambhava must have been familiar with deities and their use as embodiments of human and Buddha-like characteristics. On a mission to establish Buddhism, he appears to have embarked upon a creative strategy, so in sync with the Middle Path approach, of assimilating existing Bon deities in the Tantrayana pantheon and giving them Buddhist characteristics and meanings.

According to legend, Padmasambhava negotiated with the Bon deities and recruited many as defenders of the dharma in Tibet. An example is a 'deal' between him and the deity Pe-Har according to which, the latter agreed to renounce his demands of sacrificial blood sacrifices, and agreed to accept the egoism of the Tibetan people. Lesser deities, such as *dakinis,* female spirits, became message-givers of the dharma. The terrible, vengeful aspects of these deities came to represent the presence of such emotions in the human mind, and their worship a way of becoming aware of these aspects within the self. Thus the cohesion that Padmasamabhava was able to achieve was remarkable in its giving a Buddhist tantric wash to existing beliefs – an example of Buddhism's brand of non-violent conquest.

IN THE FOOTSTEPS OF THE BUDDHA

Our journey into Buddhism began from the path the Buddha found for himself, and it must now lead us back to his footsteps. Wherever he walked the earth, it is believed that his voice never really fell silent; indeed its echo is still discernible in the remains, one only has to hear closely enough. For the contemporary seeker, the pilgrimage into Buddhism, no matter where it begins or from which perspective it flows, almost always tends to lead to the places where the physical path is also the spiritual, where visible traces exist till today of the Buddha and his dharma.

The Buddha is said to have spoken of his own search as an uncovering of an ancient way that had been trodden by previously awakened ones, rather than position himself as someone unique, or a founder. The path, in that sense, is one that deepens with treading it, and in visiting places connected with the Buddha's life, one is literally making contact with the ground the Buddha walked on. It may be useful to remember the old analogy – of the pilgrimage as a metaphor for self-discovery, and that for many a practitioner, a visit to the places connected with the Sakyamuni helps establish a ground to their understanding of Buddhism.

ON THE TRAIL

The Buddhist pilgrimage would begin at Lumbini, in south Nepal, where Siddhartha was born. The fifth-century Chinese pilgrim Fa-Hsein described Lumbini as a 'garden' where Siddhartha's mother bathed and gave birth. Here, excavations have revealed mounds, stupas, and a well-preserved bathing pool, and an Ashokan pillar erected c. third century B. C. proclaims Ashoka's visit to the Buddha's birthplace. In recent decades, Theravada and Tibetan monasteries have been built here and plans are afoot to transform Lumbini into a 'site of peace' within an international 'Buddhist zone'.

TOP: (See page 13.)

BOTTOM: A remarkable Gandharan narrative sculpture, c. 2nd-3rd century, found in Loriyan-Tangai, a site in the former North West Frontier Province (NWFP), Pakistan. It presents a compact view of the Miracle at Sravasti. In the centre the Buddha is seated on a lotus stool of elegant design, in a niche formed by double pillars. While he is teaching, on either side is a divine attendant. There are interesting architectural and decorative elements which add to the charm. Strong Greco-Roman influences signify that perhaps the sculptor was of foreign origin.

FACING PAGE: Lama facing Sarnath.

The Great Miracle of Sravasti. Discovered in the Peshawar region, now in Pakistan, this Gandhara sculpture, belonging to the Kushana period, c. A. D. 1000, is an example of the piety of the donors who commissioned such works at the time. Gazers raise their hands to their mouths in awe and astonishment at the Sakyamuni gliding over the torrential waves, while flames emit from his shoulders.

Masterful and conceptually brilliant, this manifestation of Cakrasamvara is an important tantric bronze by a Kashmiri artisan. The god tramples Bhairava with his left foot, and rests his right foot on Chamundi/Kali in *alidhasana*. His primary hands are in *vajrahamkara mudra*, holding thunderbolts. Wearing a garland interspersed with skulls, his four heads display a figure of Tathagatas. A half crescent moon can be seen on the right top, behind which an elephant stands. A lotus petal base completes this c. mid-9th-mid-10th century Vipala piece.

Head of a bodhisattva from Java, c. 13th or 14th century. Reproduced from A. R. Coomaraswamy's *Selected Examples of Indian Art* (now out of print), 'the stupa in the headrest suggests the bodhisattva as Manjushri'.

BOTTOM: In a most unusual posture is this aspect of the bodhisattva Avalokiteshvara, sculptured in the typical red mottled sandstone of the Mathura workshops. Poised on a bench in a posture of ease, the bodhisattva sits in meditation. All the details are notable, especially the typical footwear. His identification is confirmed by the presence of the Amitabha Buddha in the front of his fan-shaped headdress. The sculpture dates to c. 2nd-early 3rd century.

Kapilavastu, the capital of the Sakya republic, was where Siddhartha spent his early life. The city that Buddhist scriptures describe as bustling with trade and imbued with material prosperity had become a 'great scene of empty desolation' by the time Fa-Hsein visited it. Today, the actual location of Kapilavastu is controversial, with both India and Nepal claiming it to be located on their soil. The debate seems to be spurred as much by the need for historical authenticity as for the ownership of the Buddha, and of the Buddhist tourism market. Both claimants, Piparva in India and Tilaurakot in Nepal, have evidence of a Buddhist presence in the form of ruins and stupas. Perhaps both were significant in some way or other in the Buddha's life.

Bodhgaya, in the Indian state of Bihar, is the site of ancient Uruvela, where the Buddha realised his nirvana. Considered the most sacred of all sites connected with the Buddha, Bodhgaya is today an international pilgrimage destination, having acquired all the accoutrements of a busy Indian temple town like *dharamshalas,* rest houses, blaring loudspeakers, and a bright, carnivalesque atmosphere. After eight centuries of being a Hindu shrine, Bodhgaya's main temple was reclaimed by the Mahabodhi Society on behalf of Buddhists in 1949. Even today, the Mahabodhi temple is governed by a joint body of Hindu priests and Buddhist monks – a characteristic middle path approach to conflict resolution. A remote descendant of the *bodhi* tree under which the Buddha sat during his nirvana can be seen here, the original having become a casualty of the twelfth century Buddhist decline and Hindu revival.

In the Barbar Hills, a little distance away from Bodhgaya, Ashoka excavated caves in the tenth year of his reign. These caves are believed to be the first evidence of Buddhist cave temples in the country.

After the enlightenment at Bodhgaya, the Buddha went to Sarnath, just north of the ancient Indian city of Varanasi, where he was persuaded to begin articulating what he had learnt. The Deer Park, which exists even today, was where the Buddha first spoke about his experience of ascetic rigours to his five former companions. The fifth-century Dhamekh stupa is supposed to mark that very spot in the park. It is here that the lion capital of an Ashokan pillar was excavated. It came to be the emblem of the modern Indian state and is now preserved in the museum there. Sarnath has also become host to a thriving Buddhist community. The Institute for Tibetan Studies located there gives a contemporary aura to this ancient place of learning.

The Buddha spent his entire post-nirvana life walking and teaching, except for the *vessa*, monsoon, retreats when the torrential rains made it impossible to travel. Sravasti, also in Bihar, was where the Buddha is believed to have spent several *vessas*. Capital of the kingdom of Kosala, Sravasti still has ruins of three monastic complexes, probably examples of the socially engaged structure of early Buddhism, where the renunciates lived in close proximity with the laity with whom they had a symbiotic relationship. Sravasti also has a site that claims to be the famed Jetavana grove, donated to the Buddha and his wandering companions by the lay disciple Anathapindika. The tree-filled Jetavana was the site of several of the Buddha's important sermons.

LEFT: Among the many residual artifacts which continue to be discovered from villages and the property of landowners, are stone sculptures. This disjointed sculpture, part of the Bharhut Stupa, is preserved in the National Museum, New Delhi. Only a part of it is shown here. The rough surface on the front suggests the rugged surface of the hill side, into which the masons are excavating, tunnelling out a cave grotto. The rocks shown on either side are geometrical outlines symbolic of the determined hewing of the rock surface by masons. They hammer into the surface metal pegs, on which they are able to balance their feet.

Rajgir, which lies 80 kilometres from Bodhgaya and is situated amidst a circle of hills, is significant as a site of teaching. This is the place where the Buddha is believed to have given the discourses that were later codified as the *Prajnaparamita* and *Lotus Sutras*. This probably happened at Vulture's Peak, a somewhat dramatic rocky outcrop on which is carved a rectangular platform to sit and teach. Rajgir is also one of the places where the great Jain teacher, Mahavira, a contemporary of the Buddha, taught. Today, Rajgir is as much a place for Buddhist pilgrimage as it is for the followers of Jainism.

Buddha died at the age of eighty – it is believed of dysentery – brought on by eating an offering of bad food at Kushinagar. The *Mahaparinibbana* temple there houses a statue of a prone Buddha lying on his side to meet his approaching death in silence. There are also remains of an imposing Ashokan stupa that was built close to the spot where the Buddha was cremated. A large archaeological park has also been built in the area.

ART AND ARCHITECTURE

The actual path the Buddha circumscribed during his lifetime was limited to areas of north and east India. However, his virtual footsteps mark all the places where Buddhism travelled, and continues to journey to. Most of these places are marked with tangible signs of the presence of Buddhism, in the form of time-enduring art, sculpture and monuments.

The story of Buddhist art is really that of Buddhism's journey through Asia. This is evident everywhere, from the 35-metre Buddha statues at Bamiyan, Afghanistan, to the second-century Ajanta cave paintings in central India; from the eighth-century temples at Borobudur, Java, to the thirteenth-century Japanese Zen gardens, the giant Buddha statues at Polonnaruwa, Sri Lanka, and Kamakura, Japan; and the splendid *thangkas* of Tibet. Each carries in itself the impress of the kind of Buddhism that gave

Seated Buddha, Sarnath, 5th century. The hands of the figure are in the *dharmacakra mudra*, the teaching gesture. This gesture is usually interpreted as the Turning of the Wheel of Dharma. The hands are held level with the heart, while the thumbs and index fingers form circles.

PAGES 114-115: Lamas with umbrellas and drums.

birth to it, for, as we know, there came to be several kinds of Buddhism, each retaining the inner core of the Buddha's teachings, yet differing in practice.

The earliest monuments and caves reflect the austerity of early Buddhism, and its insistence on the forbiddance of visual representations of the Buddha. This was in all probability a safeguard against the deification of the Buddha, since it is the easiest thing to begin worshipping a venerated teacher, and which is what happened later. But for the first four centuries after his death, the Buddha as a human form was absent from art, although his presence was at times indicated by symbols like a lotus, footprints, or the Wheel of *Dhamma*.

Gradually, the human need for expression through prayer, worship and ritual began to be felt in Buddha's dharma. This has often been called a combination of 'characteristically Indian' attitudes – the tendency to pay elaborate respect to great men, and an emotional desire to surrender oneself in self-abnegating bhakti, adoration. Indian history is replete with examples of cults of *bhagavatas*, adored ones, mostly historical figures that subsequent generations invested with divine qualities and began to worship.

The lower portion of a four level pillar rescued from the Bharhut site, Madhya Pradesh, c. 2nd century B. C. In an appealing composition it shows a group of celestial musicians playing harps and cymbals, while others clap and sing. The standing figures are graceful dancing *apsaras*. A small boy accompanies them in the foreground. Below (not seen in this image) is a Brahmi inscription naming them as Misrakesi, Subhadra, Padmavati and Alambusa. The occasion is taking place in the heavenly court of Indra.

An *apsara*, celestial nymph, in a grotto cave monastery XVII Ajanta, c. 6th century. The portrayal of heavenly beauties is an outstanding feature of the Cave paintings at Ajanta. The artist who orchestrated this painting, took pains to elaborate her unusual headgear, which seems to have a somewhat circular shape and is decorated with flowers. A chic hat is placed at a jaunty angle. Also beautifully arranged is a pearl necklace, and an elaborate jewelled necklace.

STUPAS AND CAVE ART

Since there was no tradition of making images of Buddha in the Ashokan period, this adorational impulse manifested in the veneration of the Buddha's relics – leftover bone and ash after his body had been cremated. These relics, considered extremely sacred, had been buried in sealed multi-layered hemispherical mounds called stupas. Over time, as repositories of the Buddha's mortal remains, stupas became sites of Buddhist pilgrimage and began to be adorned with artwork that was initially symbolic but became increasingly intricate with time.

Two of the earliest and finest stupas are at Sanchi and Bharhut in central India. The Sanchi stupa was built in the third century B. C. Over the next few centuries, additions were made to the simple structure in the form of carved gates and railings. So by the fifth century A. D., lay Buddhists and monks could, while performing ritual circumambulations around the stupa, contemplate Jataka narratives (stories of the Sakyamuni's previous lives as a bodhisattva), Hindu-Buddhist deities, even exquisite female nature spirits that crowd the *toranas*, gate pinnacles. It is important to note that stupa worship was independent of sects.

With the evolvement of the Mahayana sect, Buddhist art became elaborate, and in a way more sensuous. We see this in the second-century

Many aspects of the seated Buddha preaching below the *bodhi* tree are highly imaginative. The leaves of the tree are displayed as a fringe at the top, and as the sculpture is viewable from both sides, the tree is sculptured on the reverse side (not seen in the picture). Garland bearers are an additional touch, lending regality to the situation. Hand raised in the *abhay* gesture of preaching, the serene Buddha is seated on a low throne supported by lions, accompanied on either side by attendants. This Kushana sculpture, c. 1st-2nd century, is in mottled red sandstone.

A rare mural painting portraying the bodhisattva Padmapani from Bagh Cave No. 4, Gupta period, early 5th century. The portrait has a certain primitive quality in its draughtsmanship, common to murals from Bagh.

A fragment from a railing pillar in a stupa found in Pauni, Bhandara district, in ancient Maharashtra, c. 1st century B. C. The pillar is three sided. In the central portion is a brilliant Naga *Muchalinda*, posing below two mango trees bearing fruit. A display of blossoms adds delight to the eyes. It presents a horizontal divinatory inscription in the Brahmi script: *Mucarido Naga, Naga Muchalinda*. Another vertical inscription reads *Mahayasa amtevasiniya – valiya danam*, Gift of the Amtevasini Mahayasa.

Ajanta caves, which were probably used by *bhikkus* as *vessa* retreats. The twenty-odd Ajanta caves contain what is perhaps some of the most breathtaking art ever produced. Their walls are alive with a profusion of colour, forms and stories, and a mingling of the human, the divine and the natural in glowing reds, blues and greens. One of the most famous Ajanta paintings is that of Padmapani, the lotus-bearing bodhisattva of compassion, in a sublimely graceful posture.

The first actual Buddha-*rupas*, Buddha figures, appeared in Gandhara in northwest India (now Afghanistan). Interestingly, the way the Buddha is depicted in the Gandhara images has prompted many scholars to assume that these have been fashioned in the manner of Greek art. The main reasons are their aquiline features, heaped curls and toga-like garments. What could also have happened, though, is that the Gandhara artists

depicted the Buddha in their own likeness. In later centuries, royal patrons constructed great temple complexes and Buddha statues in the areas where Buddhism had spread. Many of these survive and are prayed in even today, such as the spectacular mandala-shaped Borobudur temple complex in Java, the Angkor Thom temple in Cambodia, the Wat Phra Kaeo Temple in Thailand, the Swayambhunath stupa built by Ashoka in the Nepalese capital of Kathmandu, among others.

JAPANESE ZEN

It is perhaps in Zen more than anywhere else that a well-formed aesthetic discipline based on Buddhism evolved. Art inspired by Zen is not symbolic in the way other Buddhist art, or for that matter most religious art, is. Not only is the subject matter mostly secular, its supposedly exalted subjects, such as the Masters or even the Buddha himself, are treated in the most down-to-earth, un-deified manner. Furthermore, Zen art is not representational; there is no duality between the natural and human elements. Zen master Sabro Hasegawa goes to the extent of calling Zen art a 'controlled accident', implying a certain 'artlessness' of technique.

Seeking to bring forth the 'form of emptiness and the emptiness of form', Zen aesthetics elevated even daily chores, like drinking tea for instance, and sports like archery, to art forms to be practised with skilful ease and mindfulness. In art and everyday life, the ideals of *wabi-sabi*, ordinariness-quietness, were taken to be a measure of timeless beauty, reflected in the Zen story of the cherishing of an old, cracked teacup by a Master over new, gilded ones offered by the emperor. This chastity of taste is evident in all aspects of Zen life: in the elegant but stern lines of buildings; the careful spacing of each stone in the Japanese garden; even in the spartan interiors of traditional Japanese homes.

Effortlessness in the making of art, and indeed in performing life's

TOP LEFT: The most ancient rock-cut architecture in India is a group of caves on the Barabar hills near Gaya on the Nagarjuni hills. The caves were dedicated by Ashoka and his successor to the Ajivika monks. They were tunnelled into the rock, and the walls polished brilliantly. The excavation of the Lomasa Rishi cave shows a ribbed horseshoe arch, with elephants parading around. This cave dates to the Mauryan period.

TOP RIGHT: The donor couple stands astride the entrance to Chaitya Cave III, c. 2nd century A. D. Located at Kanheri, Mumbai, Maharashtra, there is an inscription naming the donor couple.

BOTTOM: A Nepalese image of the Buddha Amitabha, his left hand in *dhyana mudra,* holding the medicine pot, and his right hand in *dharmacakra mudra.*

mundane chores, is something that cannot be practised like a craft; it would only come by letting go of the 'purpose' of doing something, and simply flowing with it. So although in Zen archery, the skill is very important, it must be forgotten in the instant of shooting, so that mind, bow, arrow, the act of shooting, all become one. Similarly in art, for instance, to make the famous bamboo paintings, the artist spent years drawing bamboos, until he was saturated with his subject. Then the art that flowed was the essence of bamboo, the direct experience of reality and the 'bambooness' of bamboo. The artist was the picture, and the picture the artist.

A similar spirit pervades the Zen haiku – a poem in seventeen syllables that must point to a certain wholeness of perception. The poet's skill is judged by his imperceptibility in the haiku, which must capture the essence of the moment in which it is conceived and written.

An example of a famous haiku by the Zen master Basho:
An ancient pond
A frog jumps in
Plop!

Another one, also by Basho:
You light the fire:
I'll show you something nice –
A great ball of snow!

Haiku of a quiet, desolate sabi-laden moment by Gochiku:
On a withered branch
A crow is perched,
In the autumn evening.

TOP LEFT: A Buddhist image in Thailand.

TOP RIGHT: Details of the Descent of Amida, silk painting portraying two groups of musicians accompanying Amida to gather up the soul of the departed.

FACING PAGE: Frescoes illuminate the dark walls of the ancient Tabo Monastery in Spiti.

BOTTOM: Maitreya, 'the benevolent messianic saviour, yet to come,' c. 2nd century A. D., Uttar Pradesh-Bihar.

PAGES 122-123: Half-brother of the Buddha, Nanda was mourning the loss of his wife Sundari. To divert his mind, the Buddha used his supernatural power to take Nanda to heaven. Once there, Nanda's desires were aroused by the beautiful celestial nymphs. The Buddha told him that he must meditate to fulfil his desire. On doing so, Nanda's desire for the nymphs disappeared. The *apsaras* are seen here under an Ashoka tree with flowers.

Nalanda, Bihar. The Palas, Protectors, a Buddhist dynasty of Bengal and Bihar, extended strong support to educational institutions. During 745-80, Gopal founded the celebrated University of Odantapura. His successors Dharmapala and Devapala founded the educational centres at Vikramashila and the important university at Somepura, respectively.

BOTTOM: Standing Buddha, Sri Lanka, part of a rich heritage of Buddhist monuments dating to the time when Ashoka delegated his son and daughter to spread Buddhism in the island.

FACING PAGE: The triple architrave of the northern *torana*, Sanchi Stupa, 3rd century B. C.

A poignant one written by Issa, on the heartbreaking hollowness of the world:

This dewdrop world –
It may be a dewdrop,
And yet – and yet –

The art that arose from the bedrock of Zen in Japan was profoundly simple and shorn of embellishment. From monochrome brush and ink paintings to beautiful bamboo ones, what is in evidence is the Zen artist's masterful use of space. Seemingly drawn from the Buddhist ideal of the emptiness at the heart of every worldly phenomenon and process, Zen-inspired paintings are precise and silent, and in most, the mere hint of form is sufficient.

SITES AND MONASTERIES

Some of the oldest Buddhist sites outside India are in Sri Lanka. Ashoka's son, *bhikku* Mahinda, who brought Buddhism to Sri Lanka, also imported several relics from India. According to chronicles, these included the Buddha's alms bowl, collarbone and his tooth, the last of which is preserved in the famed Temple of the Tooth in Kandy. Several stupas, known as *dagaba*, dot Sri Lanka, the oldest one of which is Thuparama Dagaba at Anuradhapura in north-central Sri Lanka, that houses the collarbone relic. In fact, Anuradhapura was the ancient capital of the Sinhala and ruins of some of the oldest stupas and monasteries were found there when it was

TOP: Throughout the Kalachakra initiation ceremony in Sarnath, pilgrims light butter lamps around the Dhameka Stupa. The lighting of the lamps may be an offering on one's own behalf or for others. The lamps are also a reminder for all of the light of dharma shining and reaching out to all sentient beings.

BOTTOM: A reliquary stupa, dating to the early Kushana period, mid-1st century B. C. to the 1st century A. D. Made of gray stone schist, it was gilded. Such sealed reliquaries were venerated on special occasions that marked the commemoration of important events. In between, they were housed in the monastery that looked after their maintenance. The design here is that of the standard early stupas: a circular base, topped by a dome, from which arises a square podium. Above this rises the mast with its five umbrellas that decrease in size as they ascend.

FACING PAGE: Brass and stone Buddhas.

disinterred in the early twentieth century. This is also where Sanghamitra's *bodhi* tree, a direct descendant of the Buddha's *bodhi* tree, is planted. Life has returned to the ancient city, with thousands of devotees flocking to it during festivals. Another site of great significance is Polonnaruwa in northeastern Sri Lanka, which has one of the most magnificent sights in the world – an immense reclining Buddha close to his *parinirvana*, with Ananda standing by the side.

Many ancient south-east Asian monuments were destroyed during the several wars. This makes the ones that managed to survive all the more precious. One such is the Wat Phra Kaeo Temple in Bangkok, which houses the Emerald Buddha, a figure of national importance in Thailand and for the Thai people, a symbol of the bond between the sangha and state. Thailand also has magnificent stupas at Ayutthaya, built with characteristic Thai 'lotus bud' domes. The temples at Ayutthaya, are a combination of medieval Khmer design and *shikharas,* pinnacles of south Indian temple architecture.

Cambodia has, along with the famed Hindu Angkor Wat, the twelfth-century Buddhist Angkor Thom temple complex, built by the Khmer 'god-king' Jayavarman VII after his conversion to Mahayana. The central deity here is Lokeshvara, god of the world, portrayed as the divine self of the king. Conceived as a model of the Buddhist universe, Angkor Thom has at the centre of an immense complex of shrines the great multi-towered Bayon Temple, representative of Mount Meru, axis of the universe.

Nara in Japan remains one of the great centres of East Asian Buddhism. Kyoto is the 'Zen capital of the world', with its rock gardens that are uniquely Zen, and monasteries where Zen is still taught and practised.

Apart from the places connected with the Sakyamuni's life, India has also emerged as an important centre for Tibetan Buddhism after His Holiness the Dalai Lama, along with his government-in-exile, settled in Dharamsala, Himachal Pradesh. There has been an attempt to rehabilitate some of the destroyed Tibetan monasteries by rebuilding them in India. An example is the seat of the Gyalwa Karmapa, head of the Karma Kagyu sect, rebuilt at Rumtek in the northeastern state of Sikkim.

In spite of the Chinese Cultural Revolution and the large-scale destruction of monasteries, Tibet continues to house some of the oldest and largest monasteries in the Buddhist world, such as the Jokhang, Samye, Sera and Drepung monasteries. Although some of these remain living monasteries, others, like the Dalai Lama's Potala Palace in the capital Lhasa, have been turned into museums for tourists.

FESTIVALS AND CELEBRATIONS

Around the world, Buddhists of all hues and persuasions celebrate festivals and commemorate special days. While a majority of these are cultural, some are rooted in Buddhist mythology, like Vesak, known as Vaisakh Puja in India, which commemorates at one go the birth and enlightenment of the Buddha. It is usually held on a full-moon day in the month of May. It is important to note here that almost all Buddhists, barring the Japanese, use the lunar calendar while determining the dates of festivals, so there is no one fixed date for them.

Full-moon days have come to acquire a special place in Buddhist cultures, probably due to the Buddha's birth and nirvana having occurred

ABOVE: An early bust from Afghanistan, Gandhara period, shows the Buddha enhanced in his glory by a great halo. This aspect is asserted by flames rising out of his shoulders. If the figure was complete, he would be shown walking on water, one of the miracles widely sculptured then.

TOP: A contemporary art decoration on the side wall of a monastery. After preaching the dharma to his mother, who ascended to heaven after her death, the Buddha, walking on clouds, descends from the *Tushita*, Heaven of the Thirty-Three Gods, the last paradise in heaven.

under a full moon. His first sermon in Sarnath and his *parinirvana*, death, occurred on the full moon. In most Theravadin societies, for instance, every full-moon day is an 'observance day' called *Uposatha*, and is meant as a day of reminding oneself of the Sakyamuni and his teachings. The Sri Lankan version of this is called *Poya*.

It has often been wondered by those who brand Buddhism as 'dry philosophy' whether it was capable of having or fostering any sort of festivity at all. To answer this doubt, it is sufficient to recount a fragment of a conversation between the Buddha and Ananda. Ananda asks about spiritual life, and whether it could be half composed of association with all that is beautiful. The Buddha's reply is unequivocal: this association is to be the whole, and not half, of the life of those who tread the noble eightfold path.

Thai artists have a fascination for decorating the walls of their monasteries with exceptionally attractive murals, depicting contemporary scenarios full of lively action.

BOTTOM: Katmandu in Nepal boasts many Buddhist monuments and bronze sculptures of the Buddha in various *mudras*.

PAGES 128-129: The Abbot of Wangdi Phodrang in Bhutan presides over the annual *Tsechu* rituals. On this occasion, a giant tapestry depicting Guru Padmasabbhava is unfurled over the ramparts of the Dzong.

THE UNCHANGING GROUND

Even as ancient sites and relics continue to provide the ground in which the Buddha's *dhamma* is rooted, its continuing journey in the contemporary world has attempted to provide it with the wings to rise above its own ossified conventions. It is perhaps due to the spirit of constant questioning and reasoning bred by the Buddha's exhortation to follow one's own path that new and varied interpretations of the dharma have existed at each point in time, even as they do today. In the modern world, its renewed impulse has found expression in so many different ways

TOP: Rahula, the young acolyte. Wall painting from Balawaste, central Asia, 7th century A. D. It is said that the Buddha returned home after achieving nirvana and inducted some family members into the sangha. His son, Rahula, is believed to be one of those who took refuge in the Buddha's path.

BOTTOM: A sense of humour prevails in this round medallion relief from the Bharhut Stupa. Happy-go-lucky ducks swim around in the lotus pond. They are busy pecking their bills into the lotus blossoms to gobble up insects. In the centre, a portrait of a fine-looking young man about town looms out of lotuses.

PAGES 132-133, BOTTOM: The Buddhist Triad, Jhewari, Chittagong district, latter part of the 10th century. Seated (from left to right) are Akshobhya, Vairochana and Amitabha. They are symbolic of the *triratna* –the Buddha, dharma and the sangha. The central image is seated on a double-petalled lotus. Vertical and horizontal crossbars are visible at the back. Though each image has its own halo, they are connected with stays.

– in human beings, their lives, their art and their ways of expression. So while those who tread the Buddha's path continue to visit and worship sites of his birth, nirvana and death, they are also participants in an incessant evolution of newer pilgrimages. For whether it is a giant stupa in the USA, re-established Tibetan monasteries in India, conferences exploring common ground between science and Buddhism, or one's own heart with lovingly nurtured seeds of compassion and their expression in social engagement, a quiet mind, free and fearless in its awareness – the dharma continues to manifest in many forms and speak in varied voices.

SIR AUREL STEIN

In the early1900s, Sir Marc Aurel Stein, a British archaeologist, set out to confirm his theories about the rich past of the Silk Road. By this time, the Silk Road had transformed from a path of cultural exchange to a subject of historical investigation. Scholars looked for proof of the trade and wealth of the Silk Road as described by travellers such as Xuan Zang and Marco Polo. Travellers on the Silk Road in the 1900s were mainly archaeologists gathering relics and documents that spoke of the once vibrant cultures along the route.

LEFT: Sketch of the Buddha.

BELOW: Maitreya, the future Buddha, 13th century, China. It was believed that 5000 years after the death of the Buddha Sakyamuni, the bodhisattva Maitreya would propagate the teachings of Buddhism, which would by then have been forgotten. In a seated pose, with legs crossed at the ankles, his headdress is adorned with broaches. He wears a pearl necklace with a pendant. Donning a dhoti, two scarves are draped across his chest and shoulders. There is a perfect rhythmic balance between the space between his knees , elbows and shoulders. The visage is graceful and peaceful.

Pages 134-135: Cave No. 2 in Ajanta is a *vihara*, monastery. The monks' cells and sacrarium of the Buddha, preceded by a vestibule, face onto the larger room in which twelve columns are arranged in hierarchical order with the most decorated one in the centre. Cave No. 2 is believed to be a late Mahayana *vihara* remarkable for its ceiling decorations and murals narrating the birth of the Buddha. The painted ceiling has murals as well as geometric and floral patterns. The mural scenes also include a number of stories from the Jatakas – Gautama being held by his mother and taking his first steps, and the 'thousand Buddhas' – a large painting which illustrates a miraculous story where the Buddha multiplied himself to confuse a detractor. A painted record on the rear wall of the antechamber even tells of the donation that funded the 'thousand Buddhas'.

In three expeditions, Stein traversed 25,000 miles of central Asia and western China, thus gaining the reputation of conducting 'the most daring and adventurous raids upon the ancient world'. His expeditions began with a childhood fascination with the Silk Road. He became an archaeologist and, at the age of forty, financed his first expedition into central Asia. In May 1900, Stein set out for western China and the Taklamakan Desert. This trip lasted nearly two years. In the Taklamakan Desert, Stein uncovered Buddhist paintings and sculpture and Sanskrit texts. He travelled east to Niya, where he found over a hundred wooden tablets written in A. D. 105. These tablets bore clay seals, official orders and letters written in an early Indian script. After his first expedition, other countries recognised the wealth of the Silk Road. In 1902, just two months after Stein's first expedition, Germany and Japan sought to unearth their share of Chinese treasures. As a result, an 'international race for the ancient Buddhist treasures of the Taklamakan and Gobi Deserts' began. This race involved archaeologists from seven nations and lasted over a quarter of a century. The artefacts excavated ended up in more than thirty museums across Europe, America, Russia and East Asia.

Stein set out on his second expedition, his most famous, in 1907. This trip targeted the sites of Lou Lan and Dunhuang. Stein wanted to be the first archaeologist to explore these sites. Stein reached Lou Lan

TOP: Typical decorated courtyard of a Thai monastery. A group of mythical dragons, eloquent in their stationary stance, with their large gaping jaws, seems intent on dissuading people from entering the monastery.

BOTTOM: A Tibetan aspect of Tara in copper and gilt. This highly decorated image of the beautiful and popular divinity, holds lotus stems in her hands which are poised in the *Dharmacakra Pravatna,* a *mudra* depicting preaching. This gesture is a combination of *gyanyana,* wisdom, and *vyakhyana,* explanation. The stalks rise up to the shoulder level and burst forth into exquisite lotus blossoms. She wears a glorious crown.

first, crossing the high mountains and the Lop Desert. There he found military records dated to A. D. 330. Moving on from Lou Lan, Stein stumbled upon his greatest discovery – The Caves of the Thousand Buddhas – at Dunhuang. Here he bribed Abbot Wang, leader of the monastic group in charge of the caves, and smuggled away thousands of manuscripts written in Chinese, Sanskrit, Sogdian, Tibetan, Runic Turki and Uighur. Among these manuscripts were rich Buddhist paintings and the world's oldest printed document, The Diamond Sutra, from A. D. 863.

Now viewed as a 'treasure hunter', Stein's journeys became more dangerous. The Chinese government tried to stop further expeditions and robbers watched for an opportunity to steal his discoveries. In 1915, Stein set out for his final expedition. He revisited Dunhuang and took more documents from the cave temples. He also uncovered a cemetery where the people of the Turfan region were buried. Although most of these tombs had been robbed, the objects that meant the most to Stein – the silks encasing the corpses – remained intact. The unearthing of these ancient and beautiful silks provided a conclusion to Stein's career. Stein contributed hundreds of artifacts, manuscripts and silks to the British Museum. These are now part of an important collection of items that survived the last century's upheaval in China. Some of the frescoes that Stein removed from central Asia are on view in the Aurel Stein Gallery at the National Museum, New Delhi.

MATHURA MUSEUM

Established in 1874, the Mathura Museum holds an enviable position among the museums in India. Exhibiting a rich and variegated collection of sculpture belonging to the Mathura School of Art, it has earned worldwide acclaim. Its sculptural works of great beauty, some dating back to the second century B. C., include graceful statues of the Buddha and exquisitely carved female figures, in addition to images of deities. The rich treasure of antiquarian values unearthed by Cunnigham, Growse, Fuhrer and others formed the nucleus of this museum. The collector of Mathura, F. S. Growse, founded the museum in 1874. The collections were shifted to the present building in 1930 from an old, beautifully carved, buff stone building.

Regional in character, the Museum's scope is limited primarily to the archaeological finds from Mathura and adjoining areas. The vast collection includes stone sculpture, bas-reliefs, architectural fragments and inscriptions. The Mathura School of Art, noted for its vitality and assimilative character, was a result of the religious zeal of Brahmanism, Jainism and later, Buddhism. Although mostly inspired by the early Indian arts of Bharhut and Sanchi, the influence of the Gandhara School is also evident in its sculpture. Further, it amalgamated the features of old folk cults like *yaksha* worship with later, more contemporary needs, such as those of the Buddhists, thereby creating a richly unique aesthetic style.

The Mathura Museum has the richest and by far the most important collection of Mathura School sculpture from the third century B. C. to the 12th century A. D. Perhaps the most impressive work of art displayed here is the headless life-size statue of the Mahayana Buddhist king Kanishka of the Kushana dynasty. It is the only statue of Kanishka in the world. In fact, it was during the Kushana period that the Buddha was first conceived in human form and sculpted in stone. Carved in bold relief, the features were given a three-dimensional effect, a concept probably borrowed from the West.

According to Benjamin Rowland, professor at Harvard University: 'The faces of the statues (of the Buddha sculpted during the Kushana period) are characterised by an open radiant expression; the eyes are fully open, the cheeks round and full, the mount ample, with the lips drawn into a slight smile. This smile is probably the earliest appearance of the only possible device by which the Indian sculpture could indicate the inner contentment and repose of the Buddha.' The colossal sculptural works of the Buddha, which portray a frontal stance, are masterpieces of the craftsmanship of the Mathura artists. Broad shoulders, a masculine torso and the right hand raised in *abhaya mudra* are the typical characteristics. The drapery clings to the body in fine rhythmic folds while a big designed halo adds an extra aura of divinity.

Buddhist bronze altarpiece, Sirpur, c. A. D. 800, of Tara and her attendants in three tiers. Tara, the central point of the middle tier, sits on a double lotus base supported by lions; her right hand held up in blessing, the left holding some fruit. The attendant on her right holds flowers; the one on her left holds a lotus in one hand, the other hand is held in *varada mudra*. Behind Tara, two columns support a crossbar. The highest tier portrays the seated Buddha, flanked by Maitreya on his right and Vajrapani on his left. The lowest tier displays a devotee; on either side are an adoring king and queen.

MODERN RESURGENCE

'When the iron eagle flies and horses run on wheels . . . the *dhamma* will go to the land of the red man' – so stated Padmasambhava, the originator of Buddhism in Tibet, in the eighth century.

Western interest in Buddhism is not a recent phenomenon. Long before the iron eagles of Padmasambhava's prophesy began flying, a scholarly interest had led to the translation of ancient Buddhist and Hindu scriptures into English. Enterprises like Max Muller's Sacred Books of the East and T. W. Rhys Davids' Pali Text Society presented annotated versions of the Buddhist canon even in the mid-nineteenth century. They found a captive audience in a new generation of restless experimentalists that included American thinkers Ralph Waldo Emerson, Henry David Thoreau and Walt Whitman.

Thoreau, particularly, was among the first Americans to examine a non-theistic spirituality, much in the manner of Buddhism. 'Sometimes on a summer morning, having taken my accustomed bath, I sat in my sunny doorway from sunrise till noon, rapt in reverie, in undisturbed solitude and stillness . . . I grew in those seasons like corn in the night . . . . I realised what the Buddhists mean by contemplation and the forsaking of works.'

Although such early thinkers introduced the ideas of Buddhism to the West, they had access only to scriptures. It is doubtful whether any of them actually ever met a Buddhist. While migrants from South-East Asia and the Far East introduced their Buddha and bodhisattva images and traditional practices on to Western shores, it was some time before Western practitioners began to investigate the Buddha's dharma and make it their own.

NEW BUDDHISTS

Colonel H. S. Olcott and Madame Helena Blavatsky, founders of the Theosophical Society, were the first Westerners to actually become Buddhists. They took refuge in the Three Jewels in 1880 while on a visit to Sri Lanka. Col.

TOP: (See page 13.)

BOTTOM: Samvaru embracing his consort, c. 18th century, Nepal. He stands, legs astride, in *pratyalidhasana,* the action of trampling the prostrated demonical figures, on a double lotus platform, from which emanates a fiery *prabha,* circle of stylised flames. Samvara's embracing arms hold a *vajra,* lightening bolt, and a *ghanta,* bell. His consort is in ecstasy, has her arms raised and is holding a bell with a *vajra* handle. The artistic décor is enhanced by looping circles that surround his crowned heads and a garland of human heads reaching down almost to ankle level.

FACING PAGE: Guru Padmasambhava, the founder of lamaism, was among many who came from the east to visit Nalanda, seat of Buddhist learning.

Mahaparinirvana: Complete Extinction of the Blessed One. An impressive high relief, seven metres high, this features in Grotto 26, Ajanta, Maharashtra. The grieving companions are in contrast to the dying Buddha himself. He lies on his right side, in awareness of his approaching death, observing the physical and mental changes taking place, neither grasping nor resisting. When a distraught Ananda, his prime attendant, asks him for a last piece of guidance, the Buddha responds: '*Appa dipo bhava* – Be lamps unto yourselves'. This became the cornerstone of the Buddha's path, where the practitioner was to take nothing for granted and find his way, like the Buddha had, through diligent striving and a rational, questioning attitude. Indeed, the sensibility the Buddha gave voice to at his deathbed is what has made Buddhism a radical form of spirituality for the 21st century.

Seated Sakyamuni, Kushana period, c. 3rd century. Draped voluminously, the Buddha is represented with a moustache and open eyes. The uncovered soles of his feet display lotuses. The spiked halo around the head is similar to that found in many standing figures of the Buddha. Clearly, Roman influences are visible in this sculpture.

The tradition of drawing in black marking ink on sun-dried palm leaves, is alive and well, and is the terrain of many renowned artists who have attained a special position for excellence in their craft. A part of the theme is drawn on an individual leaf and then threaded together with cotton. This pleasing portrayal of the Buddha is a worthy example of the great tradition of Orissan art.

Olcott went on to become, along with the monk Anagarika Dharmapala, one of the leading lights of the Sri Lankan Buddhist revival.

However, it was only at the end of the Second World War that the influence of Buddhism began to be felt in Europe and North America. The occupation of Japan and the wars in Korea and Vietnam led to Buddhist culture and teachings becoming available to Westerners. A two-way movement took place – the going out of inspired young people into the monasteries of Japan, Korea, Thailand and Burma and the coming to the West of Buddhist teachers. Having learned to meditate and live according to Buddhist discipline, these new Buddhists brought back experiences of long, detailed dharma study. The Chinese occupation of Tibet in 1951 resulted in the outflow of the Dalai Lama and many senior lamas into India in the late 1950s and from there, to the rest of the world.

Buddhist centres and communities were established in the West: meditation programs and retreats were routinely organised and the study of Buddhism encouraged. Some of the earliest ones were Samye Ling in Scotland co-founded in 1967 by Akong Tulku Rinpoche and Chogyam Trungpa Rinpoche; Friends of the Western Buddhist Order, also established in 1967 by the English monk Ven Sangharashita. The Theravada centre in Amaravati was set up by the American *bhikku* Ajahn Sumedho in 1984.

Later, Chogyam Trungpa, who became one of the most influential Tibetan masters in the US, founded the Shambhala centres in Colorado, Vermont and Nova Scotia, and the Naropa Institute in Colorado. The Naropa Institute is today an important place of Buddhist learning, where contemporary American Buddhist thinkers teach alongside Tibetan lamas.

THE AMERICAN SANGHA

The study and embracing of various strands of Asian Buddhism by Western seekers, and the initiation of several as *bhikkus* and lamas, was an

Monks in prayer, Temple of the Sitting Buddha, Bangkok.

BOTTOM LEFT: Kamakura Buddha, Japan.

BOTTOM RIGHT: The artist's visual dynamism lends contemporaneity to the erstwhile paintings decorating the interiors of Buddhist monuments.

FACING PAGE, BOTTOM: Adoration of the Buddha's footprints, Amaravati, 2nd century. Besotted devotees bow in adoration to the Buddha, depicted here symbolically through his footprints. The bejewelled women are obviously not initiated into the sangha. It is believed that the initiation of women began when the Buddha's stepmother, Mahapajapati Gotami, who had brought him up after his mother's death, begged to be allowed to take the vows of a renunciate. Despite the fact that the Buddha did ordain women and proclaimed them as capable of attaining enlightenment as men, the monastic sangha in Buddhist societies has not been enthusiastic about ordaining women as renunciates, probably because of their patriarchal character. Where women's monastic lineages have died out, men have actively campaigned against their re-establishment. This is beginning to change with the advent of Buddhism in the West, where feminism has been a strong influence.

outward manifestation of a Buddhist sensibility that was uniquely Western. Its earliest expression in popular culture was through the writings of a group of radical young poets in the 1950s, known as the Beat Generation. Expressing the angst of a post-war, post-Hiroshima world, poets like Gary Snyder, Jack Kerouac, Allen Ginsberg and Philip Whalen turned to Buddhism, particularly Zen, as a novel medium of voicing their quest for meaning.

The US of the 1950s and 1960s, while avidly waging the Cold War, was passionately embracing the material fruits of capitalism. With the economy on an upswing, the 'American dream' of being the land of plenty seemed realised. And yet, much like the Buddha's Kapilavastu, there was suffering in the form of dissatisfaction, ennui and meaninglessness. There was also the relentless waging of war in Vietnam and Korea, and the atmosphere of paranoia and suspicion that it engendered, again, not unlike what the great Buddhist hero Ashoka had faced. The time was ripe for another *dhammachakkapavatana*, Turning of the Wheel.

RIGHT: An ennobling artistic imagery portraying the road to nirvana.

BOTTOM: With clear influences of the Greco-Roman tradition, this sculpture, c. 2nd-3rd century, Pakistan, is representative of the Gandhara regions in Sirkap, Taxila, Peshawar, Bamyan, Jalalabad and Hadda. Invaders and travellers passed through these routes. The medley of architectural motifs, mouldings, columns and costumes are graceful, reflecting the people and activities of the time. The image of the Buddha in human form is sculpted with amazing feeling.

FACING PAGE: Buddhist altarpiece, Kashmir, c. 8th century. Kashmiri iconography of Buddhist bronze figures has its own distinctiveness. This altarpiece is supposed to be the most elaborate bronze sculpture made during Lalitsena's reign. The complexity, technical sophistry and detailed embellishments are noteworthy. The rocks are highly stylised.

PAGES 146-147: Colourful flags around a *chorten* send forth a litany of prayers across the Thimphu valley. Tibetan prayer flags are flown on high mountain passes, rooftops, bridges, monasteries, even in taxis! A typical prayer flag has as its central image a horse bearing three flaming jewels (symbolic of the Buddha, dharma and sangha) on its back. This horse, known as a 'wind-horse', lends the flags their Tibetan name, *lung-ta*. Around the horse are twenty-odd mantras. The belief is that when the wind passes over the flag, it becomes sanctified by the mantras and is beneficial for all people around. Prayer flags are printed from wooden blocks on to coloured cotton, the five colours being blue, white, red, yellow and green. They are usually renewed each Tibetan New Year.

There arose in the 'land of the red man', a thirst for an abiding truth beyond war, crass consumption, and the diktats of power and money. It was a search spun of the same warp and woof as the quest that had led Prince Siddhartha away from his life of luxury. The thirst was gratified by the arrival of a succession of Japanese Roshis, Tibetan lamas and Theravadin *bhikkus* on American shores. The Buddha's *dhamma* found ready ground again, and continued to send forth its message of peace and compassion.

Japanese Zen masters were among the first to begin teaching in the US. D. T. Suzuki, whose books inspired great interest in Zen and introduced it to innumerable Americans, arrived in the US at the beginning of the twentieth century. His initial years were spent translating important Japanese texts into English. He later taught at Columbia University, where the composer John Cage and writers Alan Watts and Alan Ginsberg were among his students.

TOP: The 1000-year-old Tabo Monastery in the Spiti valley is remarkable for its well-preserved sculptures and frescoes.

ABOVE: *Bhagavata Konigamenasa Bodhi – bodhi* tree of the Buddha Kanaka Muni, a pillar roundel that displays the tree being revered by devotees as a symbol of the Buddha. This famous and early sculpture, c. 3rd century B. C. is from Bharhut.

PAGES 148-149: Masked monks ready to perform *cham*, a ritual dance: Tibetan Buddhism, the most symbolic and esoteric Buddhist tradition, has a rich history of sacred dance in which every mask, costume, sound and gesture has a spiritual significance. Dance is a meditative practice; even the crafts associated with it, such as making of masks and costumes, are contemplative acts.

Scholars like D. T. Suzuki whetted the appetite for actual experience and even as their government engaged in conflicts in south-east Asia, several Americans made trips there to learn from masters who, in turn, began teaching in the US. Shunryu Suzuki-Roshi and his successor Katagiri-Roshi, who came to the US in 1958, founded the San Francisco Zen Centre in north California. Korean Zen master Seung Sahn established the first of his own centres in Providence, Rhode Island, in the 1960s. Theravada reached the US through scholars like Joseph Goldstein and Jack Kornfield, who studied it in India and Thailand. Goldstein, who studied in Bodhgaya with the Theravada scholar Anagarika Munindra, returned to the US to jointly found the Insight Meditation Centre in Massachusetts.

In this manner a great interest in meditation was generated among Americans. Along with yoga, meditation is now acknowledged worldwide as an effective way of dealing with the stresses and strains of modern living. Today, many turn to Buddhism to calm their minds and ease their anxieties.

As had happened earlier, when Buddhism arrived in the West, there sprang up a dialogue between the ancient faith and the twin shibboleths of modern Western thought – psychology and science. Psychology and psychotherapy had been established as important ways of understanding and dealing with the human mind in a post-Freudian world. As Buddhist philosophy passed into the public domain, with translations of Buddhists scriptures and the rise of an American sangha, several psychologists were enamoured by this ancient 'science of the mind'.

Like psychology, Buddhism spoke of the mind and consciousness. In 1934, Carl Jung had said that Zen and psychotherapy had a common concern, namely 'healing' or 'making whole'. In a serious attempt to debate

Buddha Purnima, day of both the Buddha's birth and his enlightenment, at Swayambhunath, Nepal. Five lamas, representative of the descendents of the five Buddhas, receive offerings and give blessings. They wear different coloured robes symbolic of the five elements: fire, earth, air, water and space.

BOTTOM: A finely sculptured head of the Buddha, c.3rd century, Kushana-Gandhara style.

the issue, a Conference of Zen Buddhism and Psychoanalysis was held in 1957. This marked the beginning of a connection that would later enrich the understanding of the mind for students of psychology. Ever since there has been a steady exchange leading to new approaches in therapy and a fresh perspective on the human condition.

Modern science today, is developing an idiom to dialogue with ancient philosophy, particularly Buddhism. Quantum Physics finds itself close to realising in the behaviour of sub-atomic particles, the Buddhist ideals of inherent emptiness and inter-dependence arising out of all phenomena. Even though most scientists find it difficult to accept all aspects of Buddhist thought, such as the belief in reincarnation, they are willing to examine Buddhism for points of confluence. This is due to the efforts of His Holiness the Dalai Lama and his yearly participation in the Mind and Life dialogue series, in which, for a week, scientists from various disciplines discuss the finding of a common ground between science and Buddhism.

ENGAGED BUDDHISM

In the twentieth century, Buddhist societies in Tibet, Sri Lanka, Cambodia, Vietnam and Myanmar have been torn asunder with war, internal strife, ravages of colonialism and later, of globalisation. Yet like a phoenix, there has arisen from among the ashes a new impulse, Buddhist in spirit, which has become an active agent of healing, conflict resolution and change, using as tools the lodestones of compassion, equanimity and an awareness of the overwhelming interconnectedness of life.

Since everything in the universe is co-dependent, according to the

patticcasamuppada teaching, everything is the cause of, and therefore connected with, everything else. There is an attempt today to incorporate this while dealing with issues of ecology. In south-east Asia, this movement has gained ground, with the struggle to counter the exploitative economics of globalisation merging into environmental initiatives. Says veteran Thai social activist Sulak Sivaraksa: 'The world is full of *dukkha,* the dangers of impending destruction through nuclear weapons, land and sea pollution, denial of human rights . . . . To change this, we must change ourselves first. When we cultivate ourselves towards peace and loving-kindness, Buddhism will be truly born in the hearts of men and women.'

This spirit of active involvement in society and its problems by Buddhists has come to be known as Engaged Buddhism. In fact, the discovery of the Mahayana impulse in the context of social and ecological issues has become an important part of the practice of many Buddhists in the West. Joanna Macy, Charlene Spretnak, Robert Aitken, and many others, are examining Buddhism from the activist's point of view and are trying to transmute its values into tools of constructing a global consciousness.

Yet Engaged Buddhism is not wholly new in the commonest sense of the term. The concepts of 'right livelihood' and 'right action', as spoken of by the Buddha, were pathways into engagement with society. To quote scholar Walpola Rahula: 'Buddhism arose in India as a spiritual force against social injustices, against degrading superstitious rites, ceremonies and sacrifices; it denounced the tyranny of the caste system and advocated the equality of all men; it emancipated woman and gave her complete freedom.' Ashoka's experiment with a welfare state was an example of such a policy.

Today, Buddhists like His Holiness the Dalai Lama and Vietnamese master Ven. Thich Nhat Hanh are striving to bring back a philosophy of kindness in issues connected with politics, society and the environment. The Dalai Lama, awarded the Nobel Peace Prize in 1989, has steadfastly refused to 'hate the enemy', choosing peace over war. He has often maintained that the person who wrongs you is also a human being, who also has the right to be happy. To quote him: 'If you control anger and show the opposite attitude – compassion, tolerance, patience – not only do you yourself remain in peace but the other person's anger will gradually diminish. World problems must be faced with compassion, love and true kindness. Weapons themselves cannot start a war. The button to trigger them is under a human finger, which moves by thought. The responsibility rests in thought.'

Since 1987, the Dalai Lama has been engaged in a series of dialogues between Buddhism and modern science under the aegis of the US-based Mind and Life Institute. Till 2002, ten Mind and Life conferences had taken place, centred around issues like destructive emotions; the new physics and cosmology; altruism; ethics and compassion; sleeping, dreaming and dying;

A serene beatitudinal aspect of the *Vajrasattva* in gilt-bronze, c. late 17th century. Postured in *dhyana asana* on a splendid lotus throne, his *sanghati,* robe, draped over his shoulders, has a bejewelled double border. Between his folded hands crossed in *vajrahamkara,* he grasps his symbolic *ghanta,* bell, with a *vajra* in the other hand. The lower garment is tucked into a bejewelled waist belt. He wears a conical tiara inset with semi-precious stones and lotus-petal earrings.

FACING PAGE: A 14th century painting of the Green Tara on cloth. The two trees in the background, along with the other features, suggest that this painting was created in the western part of central Tibet by Newari artists. The emphasis on blue and red is typical of their images.

'With the ever-growing impact of science on our lives, religion and spirituality have a greater role to play. There is no contradiction between the two. Each gives us valuable insights into the other. Both science and the teachings of the Buddha tell us of the fundamental unity of all things.'

Thich Nhat Hanh championed a peace movement in Vietnam during the war and continues to be the foremost voice of Engaged Buddhism today. In the manner of a latter-day bodhisattva, who defers his own nirvana to help countless suffering sentient beings, Hanh says: 'Many of us cannot see things because we are not wholly ourselves. Wholly ourselves, we can see how one person by his or her way of living can demonstrate that life is possible, that a future for the world is possible. The question: "Is a human future possible?" is meaningless without seeing the millions of our fellow humans who suffer, live and die around us. Once we have really seen them, we can see ourselves, we can see nature.'

AND THE WHEEL TURNS . . .

The renewed flowering of Buddha's *dhamma* and its globalisation has been possible because of its openness and centrality. Ultimately, it is the Buddha's insistence that 'we be lamps unto ourselves', that has given and continues to give Buddhism the creative energy to be continuously present in different cultures at different times. Just as after the Buddha's death, teachers and schools emerged, shaped by the changing concerns of the times and lands Buddhism travelled to, so too now, there exist several kinds of Buddhism around the world. Yet, they remain genetically tied to core *dhammic* realities: the axial principles of interconnectedness and interdependence; change and impermanence; compassion and non-violence to all forms of life; and the possibility of transcending suffering by overcoming afflictive emotions of greed, anger and jealousy through radical transformative insight. The wheel of *dhamma* continues to turn, attempting to take all life from ignorance and suffering into wisdom and peace.

Kushinagar, site of the Buddha's *Mahaparinirvana*. The soft glow of a candle illuminates a monk meditating beside the reclining statue of the Buddha. The reclining Buddha represents the passing of the Buddha into the great nirvana.

FACING PAGE: When Kaphina, king of Dakshinapatha, capital of Kosala, got to know that the Sakyamuni was in the vicinity and about to deliver a sermon to his devotees, he sent for his favourite elephant, and with his courtiers, set out to meet the Buddha. He was convinced that he was also destined to be a monk. It was a journey full of joy and expectancy, as depicted. On reaching the site, the king sent for his barbers and had his head shaved – a custom that is followed to this day when devotees set out on a pilgrimage. 'So did the King, and the Buddha took him into his entourage as a monk.' The Buddha, seated in *pralapadasana*, the so-called European posture, is seen surrounded by Kaphina's disciples. This 3rd century sculpture is from Nagarjunakonda in Andhra Pradesh.

BOTTOM: The Buddha in a typical post-Lichhavi Gupta style cast in fine amalgated bronze (bell metal casting), and seated gracefully on a pedestal. The sculpture has traces of gilt.

PAGES 156-157: The Chief Abbot of Bhutan, His Holiness Je Khenpo Trulku Jigme Choedar, in his chambers at the Tashichhodzong in Thimphu, as monks and royalty celebrate *Tsechu*.

Extracts from an Interview with the Dalai Lama

The Buddha of the future – Maitreya – in a Japanese rendition.

PAGES 158-159: Buddhist teachers and their sangha pray for the long life of His Holiness, the Fourteenth Dalai Lama, at the Kalachakra in Bodhgaya.

What is the goal of human life?
To be happy!

So where does nirvana fit in?
First, you need to practise basic human values. Then you can talk of nirvana, which means permanent cessation of suffering. So in a way we are back to happiness.

How can nirvana be made possible?
It is possible because it is possible to eliminate all negative emotions. The pure mind has no counterforce, and only those that have a counterforce can cease, like matter. Mind and space, too, have no counterforce and so have no reason to cease. In the case of other afflictive emotions, they might end if they have strong positive counter forces. But in the case of the mind, we cannot say that it will come to an end, as it is difficult to find a strong antidote to hinder its existence.

Here, you could argue by saying that could we put an end to compassion because it has a strong counterforce. On investigation, we will realise that kindness and love usually accompany wisdom, whereas anger and hatred might seem strong but have no basis. Everything that is good and right is the result of valid perception. Based on this, the more you analyse, the more you will be able to hold on to reality. If it is something wrong, however strong it appears, if you analyse it, its falsehood will be revealed.

Suppose you feel angry with someone. Ask yourself: 'Who is he? Is he a body or is he a mind?' You will see that there is no answer. Immediately the feeling of hatred subsides, as it has not found a target. But *karuna*, compassion, is different as it is not dependent on identifying a target. Because of this, Buddhist philosophy refers to *karuna* as the mind that does not perceive the object. *Maitri, karuna* and *bodhichitta* do not perceive the object.

How does one bring about calmness?
Through compassion. Compassion is not being kind to your friend. That is attachment because it is based on expectation. *Karuna* is when you do something good without expectations, even without knowing the other person. It is in realising that the other person is also just like me. That recognition is the basis on which you can develop *karuna*, not only towards those around you but also towards your enemy. Normally, when we think about our enemy, we think of harming him. Instead, try and remember that the enemy is also a human being and has the right to be happy just as you do.